LETTERS

TO

THE JONESES.

BY

TIMOTHY TITCOMB,

AUTHOR OF "LETTERS TO YOUNG PEOPLE," "GOLD FOIL," "LESSONS IN LIFE,"
ETC., ETC.

EIGHTH EDITION.

NEW YORK:
CHARLES SCRIBNER, 124 GRAND STREET.
1863.

JOHN F. TROW,
PRINTER AND STEREOTYPER,
50 Greene street.

PREFACE.

THERE is pretension in all works of a didactic nature, while in those which are not only preceptive, but critical of character, motive and life, there is an assumption of superiority on the part of the author which can only fail of being offensive by being ignored.

The writer of the Titcomb Series of Books has always felt this, and, however little he may have concealed himself, has hidden his head under the shadow of a *nom de plume.* The only apologics which he offers for appearing as a censor and a teacher, are his love of men, his honest wish to do them good, and his sad consciousness that his nominal criticisms of others are too often actual condemnations of himself.

Since the appearance of the author's "Letters to The Young," in 1858, he has received every year a large number of letters from their readers, asking for counsel in a wide variety of specific cases. While the present volume was not intended as a reply to these letters, it was naturally suggested by them. The author has attempted in it to present and criticise certain types of character and life, and to furnish motives and means for their improvement and reform. In order to do this successfully, it was found necessary to deal with personalities, to which it was desirable to give "a local habitation and a name;" and as the Smiths had been somewhat overworked by the literary guild, as representatives of the human race, it was determined to address the Joneses of Jonesville, who, though represented in the well-known firm of Brown, Jones & Robinson, were comparatively fresh in the field, and endowed with the average amount of "human nature."

Now, if the reader will so far favor the author as to suppose that, when a young man, he taught the district school in Jonesville, "boarding around" according to the primitive New England fashion, that he has kept himself acquainted with the lives and fortunes of his old friends and pupils there, that they have known something of him, and, through an officious representative of the family, have requested him to write them letters for the public eye, which he had no time to write for their private reading,—I say, if the reader will suppose all this, he will supply all the necessary machinery of the book, and the writer will have his justification for the direct and homely talk in which he indulges toward the family.

SPRINGFIELD, *October*, 1863.

CONTENTS.

THE FIRST LETTER.

PAGE

To DEACON SOLOMON JONES—Concerning his system of family government, ... 13

THE SECOND LETTER.

To MRS. MARTHA JONES (wife of Deacon Solomon)—Concerning her system of family government, ... 27

THE THIRD LETTER.

To F. MENDELSSOHN JONES, Singing Master—Concerning the influence of his profession on personal character, . 41

THE FOURTH LETTER.

To HANS SACHS JONES, Shoemaker—Concerning his habit of business lying, ... 57

THE FIFTH LETTER.

To EDWARD PAYSON JONES—Concerning his failure to yield to his convictions of duty, ... 71

THE SIXTH LETTER.

To MRS. JESSY BELL JONES—Concerning the difficulty she experiences in keeping her servants, ... 86

THE SEVENTH LETTER.

To SALATHIEL FOGG JONES, Spiritualist—Concerning the faith and prospects of his sect of religionists, ... 100

PAGE

THE EIGHTH LETTER.

To BENJAMIN FRANKLIN JONES, Mechanic—Concerning his habitual absence from church on Sunday, ... 115

THE NINTH LETTER.

To WASHINGTON ALLSTON JONES—Concerning the policy of making his brains marketable, ... 128

THE TENTH LETTER.

To REV. JEREMIAH JONES, D.D.—Concerning the failure of his pulpit ministry, ... 142

THE ELEVENTH LETTER.

To STEPHEN GIRARD JONES—Concerning the best way of spending his money, ... 157

THE TWELFTH LETTER.

To NOEL JONES—Concerning his opinion that he knows pretty much everything, ... 171

THE THIRTEENTH LETTER.

To RUFUS CHOATE JONES, Lawyer—Concerning the duties and dangers of his profession, ... 185

THE FOURTEENTH LETTER.

To MRS. ROYAL PURPLE JONES—Concerning her absorbing devotion to her own person, ... 200

THE FIFTEENTH LETTER.

To MISS FELICIA HEMANS JONES—Concerning her strong desire to become an authoress, ... 215

THE SIXTEENTH LETTER.

To JEHU JONES—Concerning the character and tendencies of the fast life which he is living, ... 229

PAGE

THE SEVENTEENTH LETTER.

To THOMAS ARNOLD JONES, Schoolmaster—Concerning the requirements and the tendencies of his profession, . . 242

THE EIGHTEENTH LETTER.

To MRS. ROSA HOPPIN JONES—Concerning her dislike of routine and her desire for change and amusement, . 256

THE NINETEENTH LETTER.

To JEFFERSON DAVIS JONES, Politician—Concerning the immorality of his pursuits, and their effect upon himself and his country, ... 269

THE TWENTIETH LETTER.

To DR. BENJAMIN RUSH JONES—Concerning the position of himself and his profession, ... 284

THE TWENTY-FIRST LETTER.

To DIOGENES JONES—Concerning his disposition to avoid society, ... 299

THE TWENTY-SECOND LETTER.

To SAUL M. JONES—Concerning his habit of looking upon the dark side of things, ... 310

THE TWENTY-THIRD LETTER.

To JOHN SMITH JONES—Concerning his neighborly duties, and his failure to perform them, ... 322

THE TWENTY-FOURTH LETTER.

To GOODRICH JONES, JR.—Concerning his disposition to be content with the respectability and wealth which his father has acquired for him, ... 335

LETTERS TO THE JONESES.

THE FIRST LETTER.

To Deacon Solomon Jones.

CONCERNING HIS SYSTEM OF FAMILY GOVERNMENT.

YOU are now an old man, and I do not expect that anything I shall write to you will do you good. I only seek, through what I say to you, to convey useful hints and lessons to others. It is not a pleasure to me to wound your self-love, or to disturb the complacency which you entertain amid the wreck of your family hopes. It is not delightful to assure you that your life has been a mistake from the beginning, and that your children owe the miscarriage of their lives to the training which you still seem to regard as alike the offspring and parent of Christian wisdom. If there were not others in the world who are making the same mistake that you have made, and moving forward to the same sad family disaster, you should hear from me no word that you could shape into a reproach. But you will soon pass away, with the comforting assurance that your motives, at least, were good; and to these, your only comforts, I commend you.

You were once the great man of Jonesville. You then deemed it necessary to maintain a dignified deportment, to take the lead in all matters of public moment, to manage the Jonesville church and the Jonesville minister, and to exercise a general supervision of the village. There was not a man, woman, or child in the village who did not feel your presence as that of an independent, arbitrary power, that permitted no liberty of will around it. You had your notions of politics, religion, municipal affairs, education, social life; and to these you tried to bend every mind that came into contact with you. You undertook to think for your neighbors, and to impose upon them your own law in all things. If one independent man spoke out his thoughts, and refused to be bound to your will, you persecuted him. You beset him behind and before, by petty annoyances. You took away his business. You sneered at him in public and private. In this way, you banished from Jonesville many men who would have been an honor to it, and finally alienated from yourself the hearts of your own kindred. You drove a whole village into opposition to yourself. You forced them to a self-assertion that manifested itself in a multitude of improper and offensive ways. If you opposed a harmless dance at a neighbor's house, the villagers revenged themselves by holding a ball at the tavern. It took only a few years of your peculiar management to fill Jonesville with doggeries and loafers, and to prove to you that your village management had been a sorry failure.

You seem to have conducted life upon the assumption that all the men in the world, with the single exception of Deacon Solomon Jones, are incapable of self-government. It never has occurred to you, in any dispute with a neighbor, or in any difficulty which arrayed the public against you, that you could possibly be in the wrong; and it always has offended you to think that any other Jones, or any other man, should dare to controvert your opinions, or question your decisions. And you were so stupid that, when all your neighbors—after much long-suffering and patient waiting upon your whims—rebelled against you, and went to extremes to show their independence of, and contempt for you, you attributed the work of your own hands to the devil.

Deacon Jones, the Lord gave you brains, and Yankee enterprise got you money? Had there been proper management on your part, Jonesville would be in your hands to-day; but you are aware that by far the larger proportion of your fellow citizens either do not love you, or positively hate you. How has this state of things been arrived at? Do you flatter yourself that you have been as wise as a serpent and harmless as a dove? Do you honestly believe that the loss of your influence is attributable rather to the popular than your own personal perverseness? I do not expect to make you see it, but you really did your best to make slaves of your fellows, and your fellows, recognizing you as a tyrant, kicked over your throne, and tumbled you into your chimney corner, where alone you had the power to put your peculiar theories into practice.

A man does not usually have one set of notions concerning neighborhood government and another concerning family government. You managed your own family very much as you undertook to manage your village. I can, indeed, bear witness that you gave your family line upon line and precept upon precept, but I am not so ready to concede that you trained them up in the right way. Your family was an orderly one, I admit, but I have seen jails and houses of correction that were more orderly still. An orderly house is quite as liable to be governed too much, as a disorderly house is to be governed too little.

I always noticed this fact, with relation to your

mode of family training. You enforced a blind obedience to your commands, and never deemed it necessary or desirable to give a reason for them. Nay, you told your children, distinctly, that it was enough for them that you commanded a thing to be done. You refused to give them a reason beyond your own wish and will. You placed yourself between them and their own consciences; you placed yourself between them and their own sense of that which is just and proper and good; nay, you placed yourself between them and God, and demanded that they should obey you because you willed it—because you commanded them to obey you.

It is comparatively an easy thing to get up an orderly family, on such a plan of operations as this. A man needs only to have a strong arm, and a broad palm, and a heart that never opens to parental tenderness, to secure the most orderly family in the world. It is not a hard thing for a man who weighs two hundred pounds, more or less, to make a boy who weighs only fifty pounds, so much afraid of him as to obey his minutest commands. Indeed, it is not a hard thing to break down his will entirely, and make a craven of him. I declare to you, Deacon Jones, that the most orderly families I have ever known were the worst governed; and one of these families was your own. You are not the first man who has brought up "an orderly family," and fitted them for the devil's hand by his system of government.

Now will you just think for a moment what you did for your children? I know their history, and in many respects it has been a bad one and a sad one. You governed them. You laid your law upon them. You forced upon them your will as their supreme rule of action. They did not fear God half as much as they did you, though, if I remember correctly, you represented Him to be a sort of infinite Deacon Solomon Jones. They did not fear to lie half as much as they feared to be flogged. They became hypocrites through their fear of you, and they learned to hate you because you persisted in treating them as servile dependants. You put yourself before them and thrust yourself into their life in the place of God. You bent them to your will with those strong hands of yours, and you had "an orderly family."

My friend, when I think of the families that have been trained and ruined in this way, I shudder. Your children were never permitted to have any will, and when they went forth from your threshold, they went forth emancipated slaves, and untried children in the use of liberty. When they found the hand of parental restraint removed, there was no restraint upon them. They had never been taught that most essential of all government, self-government; and a man who has not been taught to govern himself is as helpless in the world as a child. A family may be orderly to a degree of nicety that is really admirable, and still be as incapable of self-government as a family of idiots. Families that might be reckoned by thousands have left orderly homes, all prepared for the destruction to which they rushed.

The military commander knows very well that he says very little as to the moral character of his soldiers when he says that they are under excellent discipline. The drill of the camp may make the camp the most orderly of places, but this drill does not go beyond the camp, or deeper than the surface of the character. Take from the shoulders of these soldiers the strong hand of military control, and you will have—as ordinary armies go—a mass of swearing, gaming, drinking rowdies, ready to rush into any excess. The state prison is the most orderly place in the world. The drill is faultless. I know of no place where, among an equal number of men gathered from the lower walks of society, there are so few breaches of decorum; yet, when the inmates reappear in society, they are not improved. You undertook to introduce a military drill, or prison drill, or both, into your family; and you failed, precisely as generals and wardens fail. You never recognized the fact that the essential part of a child's education is that of teaching him the use of his liberty, under the control of his sense of that which is right and proper and laudable in human conduct. You did not undertake to develop and enlighten that sense at all. You managed your children instead of teaching them how to manage themselves. You never appealed to their sense of honor, or to their sense of right or propriety, as the motive to any desirable course of conduct; and when you placed your command upon one of them, and he dared to ask you after a reason, you crushed him into silence by assuring him that he had nothing to do with a reason.

It is not uncommon to hear the assertion that the sons of ministers and deacons turn out badly. Statistics show that the statement is too broad, and yet common observation unites in giving it some basis in truth. It is not at all uncommon to see the children of excellent parents—children who have been bred in the most orderly manner—going straight to destruction the moment they leave the family roof and cease to feel parental restraint. These parents feel, doubtless, very much as you do, that it is all a mysterious dispensation of Providence; but it is only the natural result of their style of training.

I know of public institutions for the reform of vagrant children, that are celebrated for the delightful manner in which those children are brought to square their conduct by rule. They march like soldiers.

They sing like machines. They enter their school-room in silent files that would delight the eye of an Indian warrior. They recite in concert the most complicated prose and verse. They play by rule, and go to bed to the ringing of a bell, and say the Lord's prayer in unison. And they run away when they can get a chance, and steal, and swear, and cheat, and prowl, and indulge in obscene talk, as of old. I know of other public institutions of this kind, or, at least, one other, that has no rule of action except the general Christian rule within it. The children are taught to do right. They are instructed in that which is right. Their sense of that which is true and good and pure and right and proper is educated, developed, stimulated, and thus are the childen taught to govern themselves. They govern themselves while in the institution, and they govern themselves after they leave it. It is impossible to reform a vicious child without patiently teaching that child self-government. All the drill of all the masters and all the reformers in the world will not reform a single vice of a single child; and this show of juvenile drill that we meet with in schools and charitable institutions is frequently—nay, I will say, generally—a most deceitful thing—the specious cover of a system of training that is terribly worse than useless. If dogs could talk, they could be taught to do the same things in the same way; but they would hunt cats and bark at passengers in the old fashion when beyond the reach of their master's lash.

You will see, Deacon Jones, that your mode of family training has introduced me to a field of discussion as wide as it is important. It relates to public institutions as well as to families, and to nations as well as to public institutions. You and I, and all the democrats of America, have been indulging in dreams of democracy in Europe, but these dreams do not come to pass, and are not likely to be realized at all. The people of Europe have been governed. They know nothing about self-government, and, whenever they have tried the experiment, they have sadly failed. That which alone imperils democracy in this country is the loss of the power of self-government, and that which alone prevents the establishment of democracy in Europe is the lack of that power. The governing classes of Europe will take good care to see that that power be not developed.

But I return to this matter of family government, and I imagine that, before this time, you have asked me whether I have intended to sneer at orderly families. I answer—not at all. There must be, without question, more or less repression of the irregularities of young life, and of such rough passions as sometimes break out and gain ascendency in certain natures; but this should be exceptional. I do not sneer at orderly families, but I like to see order growing out of each member's sense of propriety, and each member's desire to contribute to the general good conduct and harmony of the family life. I like to see each child gradually transformed into a gentleman or a lady, with gentlemanly or ladylike habits, through a cultivated sense of that which is proper, and good. I know that children thus bred—taught from the beginning that they have a stake and a responsibility in the family life—used from the beginning to manage themselves—are prepared to go out into the world and take care of themselves. To them, home is a place of dignity, and they will never disgrace it. To them, liberty is no new possession, and they know how to use without abusing it. To them, self-control is a habit, and they never lose it.

Do you know what a child is, Deacon Jones? Did you ever think whence it came and whither it is going? Did it ever occur to you that any one of your children is a good deal more God's child that it is yours? Did you ever happen to think that it came from heaven, and that it is more your brother than your child? Never, I venture to say. You never dream that your children are your younger brothers and sisters, intrusted to you by your common Father, for the purposes of protection and education; and you certainly never treat them as if they were. You have not a child in the world whose pardon you should not ask for the impudent and most unbrotherly assumptions which you have practiced upon him. Ah, if you could have looked upon your sons as your younger brothers and your daughters as your younger sisters, and patiently borne with them and instructed them in the use of life and liberty, and built them up into a self-regulated manhood and womanhood, you would not now be alone and comfortless. A child is not a horse or a dog, to be controlled by a walking stick or a whip, under all circumstances. There are some children that, like some dogs and horses, have vicious tendencies that can only be repressed by the infliction of pain, but a child is not a brute, and is not to be governed like a brute. A child is a young man or a young woman, possessing man's or woman's faculties in miniature, and is just as sensitive to insult and injury and injustice as in after years. You have insulted your children. You have treated them unreasonably, and you ought not to complain if they hold you in dislike and revengeful contempt.

You never did anything to make your children love you, and you cannot but be aware that the moment that they were removed from your authority, you lost all influence over them. Why could you not reclaim that boy of yours, who madly became a debauchee, and disgraced your home, and tortured your heart?

Because you had never made him love you, or given him better motives for self-restraint than your own arbitrary will. He had been governed from the outside, and never from the inside; and when the outside authority was gone, there was nothing left upon which you had power to lay your hand. Why did your daughter elope with one who was not worthy of her? She did it simply because she found a man who loved her, and gave her the consideration due her as a woman—a love and a consideration which she had never found at home, where she was regarded by you as the dependent servant of your will. She was nothing at home; and, badly as she married, she is a better and a freer and a happier woman than she would have been had she continued with you. I wish to impress upon you the conviction that these children of yours went astray, not in spite of your mode of family training, but in consequence of it. If I should wish to ruin my family, I would pursue your policy, and be measurably sure of the desired result.

It is not pleasant for me to tell you these things, but I am writing for the public, and can have no choice. I tell you, and all who read these words, that, if you do not get the hearts of your children, and build them up in the right use of a liberty which is no more theirs after they leave your roof than it is before, you will be to them forever as heathen men and publicans. If they take the determination to go to destruction, they will go, and you cannot save them. A child must have freedom, within limits which a variety of circumstances must define, and be taught how to use it, and made responsible for the right use of it. It is in this way that self-government is taught, and in this thing that self-government consists. All children, on arriving at manhood and womanhood, should be the self-governed companions and friends of their parents, and on going out into the world, or losing parental control, should not feel the transition in the slightest degree. No child is trained in the right way who feels, when he steps forth from the family threshold—an independent actor—any less restraint than he felt the hour before. If he does, he is in danger of falling before the first temptation that assails him.

THE SECOND LETTER.

To Mrs. Martha Jones (Wife of Deacon Solomon).

CONCERNING HER SYSTEM OF FAMILY GOVERNMENT.

I SUPPOSE I have thought of you ten thousand times within the last twenty years. I never see a clean kitchen, or a trim and tidy housewife, or an irreproachable "dresser," with its shining rows of tin and pewter, or a dairy full of milk, or a cleanly raked chip-yard, or polished brass andirons, flaming with fire on one side and reflecting ugly faces on the other, or catch a certain savory scent of breakfast on a frosty morning, or see a number of children crowded out of a door on their way to school, without thinking of you. Thriving, busy, exact, scrupulous, neat, minute in your supervision of all family concerns, striving to have your own way without interfering with the deacon's, you have always lingered in my memory as a remarkable woman. You sat up so late at night and rose so early in the morning, that it seemed as if you never slept. There was a chronic alertness about you that detected and even anticipated every occurrence in and around the house. Not a door could be opened or a window raised in any part of the house, however distant it might be, without your hearing and identifying it. Not a voice was heard within the house at any time of the day or night that you did not know who uttered it. Your soul seemed to have become the tenant of the whole building, and to be conscious of every occurrence in every part of it at every moment. You not only knew what was going on everywhere, but every part spoke of your presence.

It was a curious way you had of maintaining the family harmony without the sacrifice of your own sense of independence. You really carried on a very independent life within certain limits. You were aware that, in the matter of will, the deacon, your husband, was very obstinate, and that you could never hope to dispute his empire. So you shrewdly managed never to cross him where the course of his will ran strongest, and to be sure that no one else crossed him. I remember very well your look of amazement and reproof when you heard me treat with apparent irreverence some of his most rigidly fixed opinions, and assail prejudices which you knew were as deeply seated as his life. I enjoyed your look of amazement quite as much as I did the deacon's anger, for it seemed to me a very justifiable bit of mischief to break into a family peace that was maintained in this way. By humoring and indulging your husband, in all matters over which he saw fit to exercise authority, and by so closely attending to everything else that he did not think of it, you kept him in a state of self-complacency, and were the recognized queen of a wide realm.

As I look back upon your life, I find but little to blame you for. Wherever your errors have been productive of mischief, they have been errors of ignorance—mistakes—possibly excusable in the circumstances under which they were committed. You loved your children with all the tenderness and devotion of a good mother, but, in your anxiety that they should not cross their father's will, and provoke his displeasure, you became but little better than an irksome overseer to them. You knew that if there was anything that your husband insisted on, it was parental authority. You knew that the strict ordering of his family was his pet idea, and that family government, in the fullest meaning and force of the phrase, was his hobby. This pet idea—this hobby—you made room for in your family plans. You knew that he was often unreasonable, but that made no difference. You knew that his will ran strongest in that direction, and you made it your business to see that as few obstacles lay in its path as possible. On one side stood the deacon's inexorable laws and rules and will, by which his children, of every age, were to square their conduct. On the other stood those precious children of yours, with all the wilfulness and waywardness of children—with all their longing for parental tenderness and indulgence—with moods which they had never learned to manage, and tempers which they did not know the meaning of; and you became supremely anxious that the deacon should not be provoked by them to wrath, and that they should escape the consequences of his displeasure.

Well, what was the consequence? This ceaseless vigilance which you had learned to exercise over every portion of the household economy, you extended to the bearing and conduct of your children. You exercised over them the strictest surveillance. You carried in your mind and in your manners the dread of a collision between them and their despotic governor. You tried to save him from irritation and them from its consequences. You kept one eye on him and another on them, and nothing in the conduct of either party escaped you. Your children, as they emerged from babyhood, grew gradually into the consciousness that they were watched, and that not a word could be uttered, or a hand lifted, or a foot moved, without a degree of notice which curtailed its liberty. It was repression—repression—nothing but repression—everywhere, for them. No hearty laugh, or overflowing, childish glee, or noisy play for them, for fear that the deacon might be disturbed.

At last, every child you had, in addition to the fear of its father, came to entertain a dread of its mother. I think your children loved you, or would have loved you, had they not associated you forever with restraint. If they played, you were near with your everlasting "hush!" If they sat down at table, they knew that your eye was upon them—that you watched the position of every head under the deacon's long "grace"—the passage of every mouthful—the manner in which they asked every question and responded to what was said to them—the amount of food and drink consumed—everything. They felt themselves wrapped up in—devoured by—a vigilant supervision that took from them their liberty and their will, and with them, all feelings of self-respect and self-possession.

It is not the opinion of your neighbors that either your husband or yourself has had anything to do with the ruin of your children. The deacon was so strict and so efficient in his family government, and you were so scrupulously careful in everything that related to their manners at home and away, that they did not imagine it possible that any bad result could naturally flow from such training. I do not say that they are mistaken from any wish to blame you, but I must tell you the truth. Your minute watchfulness and censorship exercised over these children until you became to them God, conscience, and will, were just as fatal to a manly and womanly development as the deacon's irresponsible commands. A boy that feels that every word of his mouth and every movement of his body is watched by one whose eye never sleeps, and whose hand is ever ready to repress, becomes at last a coward or a bully. There are natures that will not submit to this surveillance; and when these become weary of the pressure, they kick it aside, and parental restraint—associated with all that is hateful in slavery—is gone forever.

Under the peculiar training and home influences to which your children were subjected, there were but two things that they were likely to become, viz.: rebels or cravens. Your children were naturally high-spirited, like the deacon and yourself, and they became rebels. Otherwise, they would have carried with them through life the feeling that whatever show they might put on—however much they might struggle against it—they were underlings. There are some men and some women, probably, who, living through a long life under favorable circumstances, recover from this early discipline of repression, and this abject slavery of the will, but they are few. They must be few. The negro who has once been a slave cannot, one time in ten, refuse to take off his hat or bow to a white man. He is never at home, when placed on an equality with him. He carries in his soul the badge of servility, and he can no more thrust it from his sight or banish it from his consciousness than he can change the color of his skin. This is not because he is a negro, simply, but because he has been a slave—because he has been trained up to have no will, and to be controlled under all circumstances by the wills of those who had him in their power.

A child can be made the slave of a parent just as thoroughly as a negro ever was made the slave of a white man, and such a child can be just as everlastingly damaged by parental or family slavery, as a bondman can be by any system of bondage. A child can be made as mean, and cowardly, and deceitful, and devoid of self-respect, by a system of management which puts a curb upon every action, as the devil himself could possibly desire. This system of watchful repression, and minute supervision, and criticism of every action, among children, is utterly debilitating and demoralizing. You intended no harm by it, madam. Under the circumstances, it was a very natural thing for you to do; but I think you can hardly fail to see that, unwittingly, you perfected the work of destruction in your children which the deacon so thoroughly began, and for which he would have been, without your assistance, entirely sufficient.

Oh! when will the world learn that children are neither animals nor slaves? When will the world learn that children—the purest, sweetest, noblest, truest, most sagacious creatures in the world—with a natural charter of liberty as broad as that enjoyed by the angels—should be treated with respect? When shall this idea that all legitimate training relates to the use of liberty—to the acquisition of the power of self-government—become the universal basis of family policy?

You ask me what I really mean by all this, for you are a practical woman, and are not to be taken in by a set of easily written phrases. Well, I will try to explain, or illustrate, my meaning. I remember a gathering at your house—a party of friends—to which your children were admitted; and I remember with painful distinctness the telegraphic communication which you maintained with them during the whole evening. If James got his legs crossed, or, in his drowsiness, gaped, or if he coughed, or sneezed, or laughed above a certain key, or make a remark, or moved his chair, it was: "James, h—m!"—"James, h—m!" "James, h—m!" And James was only one of half a dozen whom you treated in the same way. You began the evening with the feeling that you were entirely responsible for the behavior of those children—just as much responsible as if they severally were the fingers of your hand. You acted as if they were machines which, for the evening, you had undertaken to operate? They felt that they were under the eye of a vigilant keeper, and they did not dream of such a thing as acting for themselves. They were acting for you, and they did not know until they heard your suggestive "h—m!" whether they were right or wrong. You undertook for the evening to be to them in the stead of their sense of propriety; and the communication between them and you being imperfect, they often offended. I know that your own good sense will tell you now that this is not the way gentlemen and ladies are made.

I was recently in a family circle where I witnessed a most delightful contrast to all this—where the sons and daughters were brought up and introduced to me by the father and mother with as much politeness and cordiality as if they were kings and queens every one, and with as much freedom as if the parents had not the slightest doubt that the children—from the oldest to the youngest—would bear themselves like ladies and gentlemen. There was no forwardness on the part of these children, as you may possibly suppose; yet there was perfect self-possession; and each child knew that he stood upon his own merits. I suppose that if any one of these children had indulged in any impropriety during this interview—as not one of them did—he would have been kindly told afterward, by one of the parents, what he had done, and why he should never repeat it. Your children (pardon me for saying it) were always awkward in company, and for the simple reason that they did not know whether they were pleasing you or not. They had no freedom, and were guided by no principle. Your will was their rule, and your will, so far as it related to all the minutiæ of behavior, was not thoroughly known; so they were always embarrassed, and always turning their eyes toward you. Your entire system of management was based on distrust, while that of the family with which I contrast yours was founded on trust. Your children, while you could possibly keep your hold upon them, were never permitted to outgrow their petticoats, while those of the other family alluded to were put upon their own responsibility just as soon as possible. Is there any doubt as to which system of treatment is best?

Perhaps you, and many others who read this letter, think that parental authority cannot be maintained without its constant and direct assertion. If so, then you and they are mistaken. I have known families that possessed fathers and mothers who were honored, admired, loved, almost worshiped—fathers and mothers whose children dreaded nothing so much as to give them pain—yet these same children knew no such word as fear, and would have been utterly ashamed to render the assertion of parental authority necessary. Parents and children were friends and companions—the children deferring to the wishes and opinions of the parents, and the parents consulting the happiness and trusting the good sense and good intentions of the children. Whenever I hear a young man calling his father "the old man," and his mother "the old woman," I know that the old man and the old woman are to blame for it.

If your children had turned out well, it must have been in spite of a system of training which was so far from being education as to be its opposite. There was no inner life organized; there was no building up of character; there was no establishment in each child's heart of a bar of judgment—no exercise in the use of liberty; but only restraint, only fear, only slavery.

I do not entertain those opinions of one variety of disorderly families, which you and the deacon seem to have entertained all your lives. I have never yet seen the house where children were happy that did not show evidences of disorder; and a man is a fool, or something worse, who quarrels with this state of things. Where children have playthings, and where they play with them, there must necessarily be disorder, and furniture more or less disturbed and defaced, and noise more or less disagreeable, and litter that is not highly ornamental. And before children have had an opportunity to learn propriety of speech and deportment—before they are educated—there will be in their conduct—in playroom and parlor alike—more or less of irregularity and extravagance. Remarks will be made that will shock all hearers; laughs too boisterous to be musical will be indulged in; sudden explosions of anger will occur, with other eccentricities of conduct that need not be named. There are remedies for all these—in time. When, in the course of their education, the sense of propriety is stimulated and strengthened, and pride of character is developed, these irregularities will disappear, and an orderly family will be the consequence, each child having become its own reformer.

There was a feature of your family government (which you held in common with your husband) that made still more complete the slavery of your children. It was the deacon's opinion, you will remember, that a boy who was not too tired to play at ball, or slide down hill, or skate, was not too tired to saw wood, and it was his policy to direct all the excess of animal life which his boys manifested into the channels of industry and usefulness. You seconded this opinion, and maintained that a girl who was not too sleepy to make a doll's hat, or a doll's dress, was not too sleepy to hem a handkerchief, or darn a stocking. So your children never had what children call "a good time." Always kept at work when possible, and always restrained in every exhibition of the spirit of play, home became an irksome place to them, and childhood a dreary period. Your children were never permitted to do anything to please themselves in their own way. Everything was done—or you insisted that everything should be done—to please you, in your way. If one of your daughters sat down to rest, or resorted to a little quiet amusement, you stirred her at once by some petty command. I was often tempted to be angry with you because you would never give your children any peace. You had always something for them to do, and something that had to be done just at the very time when they were enjoying themselves the best.

"Precept upon precept" is very well, in its way, but principle is much better. The principle of right and proper acting, fully inculcated, renders unnecessary all precepts; and until a child has fully received this principle he is without the basis of manhood. The earlier this principle is received and a child thrown upon his own responsibility, and made to feel that he is a man, lacking only years to give him strength and wisdom, the safer that boy is for time and for eternity. The moment a boy becomes morally responsible, he becomes in a most important sense—a sense which you and the deacon never recognized—free. I do not say that he is removed from parental control or rational restraint, but that it is the business of the parent to educate him in the principle of self-government. A boy bred thus, becomes ten times more a man than a boy bred in the way which has seemed best to you; and when he goes forth from the parental roof he goes forth strong, and able to battle with life's trials and temptations. Children long for recognition —to do things for themselves—to be their own masters and mistresses. Their play is all based on the assumption that they are men and women, as, in miniature, they are; and, insisting on the right use of liberty, and teaching them how to use it, they should have it, restrained only when that liberty is abused.

THE THIRD LETTER.

To F. Mendelssohn Jones, Singing Master.

CONCERNING THE INFLUENCE OF HIS PROFESSION ON PERSONAL CHARACTER.

I ONCE heard the most renowned and venerable of all the professors of music in this country say that he always warned his classes of young women to beware of singing men, and, with equal emphasis, warned his classes of young men to beware of singing women. He alluded, of course, to professional singers, and I have too much respect for his Christian character to suppose that he was not thoroughly in earnest. The statement will not flatter your self-conceit, but I immediately thought of you, and the life you have led. You were what people called a bright boy. Indeed, you were what I should call a clever boy. You were quick, ingenious, graceful, skilful; and your father and mother told me, with evident pride, and in your presence, that you had a remarkable talent for music. "Felix Mendelssohn could sing," they said, "and carry his own part, before he was three years old." And Felix Mendelssohn was brought out on all possible occasions, to display his really respectable gifts as a singer, and was brought out so often, and was so much praised and flattered, that, before he was old enough to know much about anything, he had conceived the idea that singing was the largest thing to be done in this world, and that Felix Mendelssohn Jones had a very large way of doing it.

Twenty years have passed away, and where and what are you? You are a singing master, with a limited income, and a reputation rather the worse for wear. You have never been convicted of any flagrant acts of immorality, but men and women have ticketed you "doubtful." Careful fathers and mothers are careful not to leave their daughters in your company. Ladies who prize a good name above all other possessions never permit themselves to be found alone with you. There are stories floating about concerning your intrigues, and the jealousy and unhappiness of your wife. Everybody says you are an excellent singer, that you understand your business, &c., &c., but all add that you know nothing about anything else, that they would not trust you the length of their arms, that you are a hypocrite and a scapegrace, that you ought to be horsewhipped and hissed out of decent society, that it is strange that any respectable man will have you in his family, and a great many other ugly things which need not be related. I am aware that you have warm friends, but not one among the men, unless it be some poor fellow whose wife's name has been coupled with yours in an uncomfortable way. Wherever you go, there are always two or three women who become your sworn partisans—women who have your name constantly on their lips—who will not peaceably or without protest hear your immaculateness called in question—women who, somehow, seem to have a personal interest is establishing the uncompromising rigidity of your virtue. I do not think very highly of these women.

You are a handsome man, and how well you know it! You are a "dressy" man. There is no better broadcloth than you wear, and no better tailor than you employ. You are as vain as a peacock, and selfish beyond all calculation. A stranger, meeting you in a railroad car, or at a hotel, would not guess the manner in which you get your money, and least of all would he guess that in your home, where you are a contemptible tyrant, your wife sits meanly clad, and your children eat the bread of poverty.

I have asked myself a thousand times why it is that you and a large class of singing men and singing women are thus among the most worthless of all human beings. One would suppose, from the nature of the case, that you and they would be among the purest and noblest and best men and women in the world. Music is a creature of the skies. It was on the wings of music that the heaven-born song—" Peace on earth : good will to men "—came down, and thrilled Judea with sounds that have since swept around the world. It is on the breath of music that our praises rise to Him whose life itself, as expressed in the movements of systems and the phenomena of vitality, is the perfection of rhythmical harmony. It is music that lulls the fretful infant to sleep upon its mother's bosom, that gives expression to the free spirit of boyhood when it rejoices upon the hills, that relieves the tedium of labor, that clothes the phrases by which men woo the women whom they love, and that makes a flowery channel through which grief may pour its plaint. It stirs the martial host to do battle in the cause of God and freedom, and celebrates the victory; and " with songs " as well as with " everlasting joy," we are told, the redeemed shall enter upon their reward at last. Why, one would suppose that no man could live and move and have his being in music, without being sublimated—etherealized—spiritualized by it—kept up in a seventh heaven of purity and refinement.

This may all be said of music in general, but to me

there seems to be something peculiarly sacred in the human voice. There is that in the voice which transcends all the instruments of man's invention. It is one of God's instruments, and cannot be surpassed or equalled. It is the natural outlet of human passion—the opening through which—in love and hate, in grief and gladness, in desire and satisfaction—the soul breathes. It pulsates and trembles with that spiritual life and motion which are born of God's presence in the soul. It is not only the expression of all that is human in us, but of all that is divine.

One would suppose, I repeat, from the nature of the case, that you and all the professional singing men and singing women would be among the purest and noblest and best men and women in the world, but you and they are notoriously no such thing. On the contrary, you are the mean and miserable profligate I have already charged you with being, and many of your associates are like you. In saying this, I do not mean to wound the sensibilities of some singing men and women who do not belong in your set. I know truly Christian men and women who have devoted their lives to music, but they are in no danger of being confounded with your crowd and class. They despise you as much as I do, and regret as much as I do the facts which have associated music with so much that is mean and unworthy in character and conduct.

It may be interesting to the public, if not to you, to study into the causes of this wide-spread immorality and worthlessness among those who make singing the business of their lives. In your case, and in many others, personal vanity has had more to do than anything else. You were bred from the cradle to a love of praise. Your gift for music was manifested early, and your parents undertook to exhibit you and secure praise for you throughout all the years of your boyhood. You grew up with a constant greed for admiration, and this grew at last into a passion, which has never relinquished its hold upon you. You became vain of your accomplishment, and vain of your personal beauty, and vain of your whole personality. You have been singing in church all your life, and giving voice to the aspirations and praises of others, but, probably, there has never, in all that time, gone up from your heart a single offering to Him who bestowed upon you your excellent gift. You have, during all your life, on all occasions, sung to men, and not to God. As your voice has swelled out over choir and congregation, you have been only thoughtful of the admiration you were exciting in the minds of those who were listening, and have always been rather seeking praise for yourself than giving praise to your Maker.

This love of admiration and praise has been, then, the mainspring of your life; and no man or woman can be even decent with no higher motive of life than this. With this motive predominant, you have grown superlatively selfish. You refuse to share your earnings with your wife and children, because such a policy would detract from your personal charms, or your personal comforts. You quarrel with every man of your profession, because you are afraid that he will detract somewhat from the glory which you imagine has settled around you. Your mouth is constantly filled with detraction of your rivals. In the practice of your profession, you are thrown into contact with soft and sympathetic women, who are charmed by your voice, and your face, and your style, and your villainously smooth and sanctimonious manners, and they become easy victims to your desire for personal conquest. Thus has music become to you only an instrument for the gratification of your greed for admiration, and, among other things, a means for winning personal power over the weak and wayward women whom you encounter.

Life always takes on the character of its motive. It is not the music which has injured you: it is not the music which injures any one of the great brotherhood and sisterhood of vicious genius. There are those among musicians who can plead the power of great passions as their apology for great vices. No great musician is possible without great passions. No man without intense human sympathies in all directions can ever be a great singer, or a great musician of any kind; and these sympathies, in a life subject to great exaltations and depressions, lead their possessor only too often into vices that degrade him and his art. But you are not a great musician, and I doubt very much whether you have great passions. I think you are a diddler and a make-believe. I think your vices are affectations, in a considerable degree, and that you indulge in them only so far as you imagine they will make you interesting.

There is something very demoralizing in all pursuits that depend for their success upon the popular applause. We see it no more in public singing than in acting, and no more in acting than in politics. I doubt whether more singers than politicians are ruined by the character of their pursuits. A man who makes it the business of his life to seek office at the hands of the people, and who administers the affairs of office so as to secure the popular applause, becomes morally as rotten as the rottenest of your profession.

I never hear of an American girl going abroad to study music, for the purpose of fitting herself for a public musical career, without a pang. A musical education, an introduction to public musical life, and a few years of that life, are almost certain ruin for any woman. Some escape this ruin, it is true, but there are temptations laid for every step of their life. They find their success in the hands of men who demand more than money for wages. They find their personal charms set over against the personal charms of others. Their whole life is filled with rivalries and jealousies. They find themselves constantly thrown into intimate association on the stage with men who subject themselves to no Christian restraint—who can hardly be said to have had a Christian education. They are constantly acting in operas the whole dramatic relish of which is found in equivocal situations, or openly licentious revelations. In such circumstances as these, a woman must be a marvel of modesty and a miracle of grace to escape contamination. I do not believe there is a woman in the world who ever came out of a public musical career as good a woman as she entered it. She may have escaped with an untarnished name—she may have preserved her standing in society, or even heightened it, but in her inmost soul she knows that the pure spirit of her girlhood is gone.

It is the dream, I suppose, of most women who undertake a musical career, that, after winning money and fame, they shall settle down into domestic life gracefully, and be happy in retirement. Alas! this is one of the dreams that very rarely "come true." The greed for popular applause, once tasted, knows no relenting. The public life of women unfits them for domestic life, and the contaminations of a public singing woman's position render it almost impossible for her to be married out of her circle; so that a woman who spends ten years on the stage usually spends her life there, or does worse. I do not wonder at the old professor's warning against singing women, or singing men. It is enough to break down any man's or woman's self-respect to be dependent for bread and reputation upon the applause of a capricious public—to devote the whole energies of one's being to the winning of a few clappings of the hand and a few tosses of the handkerchief, and to feel that bread, and success of the life-purpose, depend on these few clappings and tosses.

I have a theory that it is demoralizing to pursue, as a business, any graceful accomplishment which was only intended to minister to the pleasure and recreation of toiling men and women. I have not read history correctly if it be not true that the artists of all ages have been generally men of many vices. There have been men of pure character among them always, but, as a class, they have not been men whom we should select for Sunday school superintendents, or as husbands for our daughters. If you, Felix Mendelssohn Jones, had been a tailor, and had worked hard at your business, and only used your talent for music in the social circle and the village choir on Sunday, and been just as vain as you are to-day, you would have been a better man than you are now, I think. I think this devotion of your life to music has had the tendency, independently of all other influences, to make you intellectually an ass and morally a goat.

Whether there is soundness in this theory or not, singing as a pursuit must come under the general law which makes devotion to one idea a dwarfing process. A man who gives his life to music—who becomes absorbed by it—and who really knows nothing else, will necessarily be a very small specimen of a man. The artist is developed at the expense of the man. Music is thrown entirely out of its legitimate and healthy relations to his life, and he makes that an object and end of life which should only minister to an end far higher. When a man undertakes to clothe his manhood from materials furnished by a single pursuit, even when that pursuit is so pure and beautiful as that of music, he runs short of cloth at once. I have no doubt that one of the principal reasons why music has such a dwarfing effect upon a multitude of those who make it the pursuit of their lives, is, that it is so fascinating and so absorbing—because it possesses such a power to drive out from the mind and life everything else. There is no denying the fact that, in the eye of a practical business man, musical accomplishments in men are regarded as a damage to character and a hinderance to success. It is pretty nearly the universal belief that a man who is very much devoted to music is rarely good for anything else. This may not be true—and I doubt whether it is strictly true—but it is true enough, and has always been true enough to make it a rule among those who have no time for nice distinctions and exceptional cases.

I do not wonder, Felix Mendelssohn Jones, that intellectually you are a dwarf. I do not wonder that men who have nerve and muscle and common sense, and practical acquaintance with the great concerns of life, and a share in the world's earnest work, should hold you in contempt for other reasons than those which relate to your morals. What did you ever study besides music? Upon what subject of human interest are you informed except music? Upon what topic of conversation are you at all at home unless it be music? Why is it that you have nothing to say when those questions are discussed which relate to the political, moral, social, and industrial life of the race or nation to which you belong? No man has a right to be more a musician than a man, and no musician has a right to complain when men who are men hold him in contempt because he is the slave of an art of which he should rather be the kingly possessor. There is a vast deal of nonsense afloat in the world about being married to music, or married to art, as if music were a woman of a very seductive and exacting character, and musicians were very gallant and knightly people who make it their business to bend before a lifted eyebrow, and follow the fickle swing of petticoats to death and the worst that follows it.

There is another cause that has operated to make you much less a man than you might have been under other circumstances, and this is almost inseparable from your life as a public singer. Your life has been a vagabond life. You, in your humble way, passing from village to village, have only had a taste of that dissipation of travel which the more famous members of your profession are obliged to suffer. From the time a public singer begins his career until he closes it, he has no home. He is never recognized as a member of society. He is obliged to be all things to all men, everywhere. He has no nationality. He shouts for the stars and stripes in New York, but would just as easily shout for the stars and bars wherever they float. He is equally at home in England and France and Italy, and salutes any flag under which he can win plaudits and provender. He has no politics, he has no religion, "to mention," he has no stake in permanent society whatever. The institutions of Christianity, public schools, educational schemes and systems, the great, permanent charities, municipal and neighborhood life—he has no share in all these. He runs from country to country and from capital to capital, or scours the country, and does not cease his travels until life or health or voice is gone. It is impossible for any man to be subjected to such dissipation as this without receiving incalculable damage of character. He can think of nothing but his profession under these circumstances. He can have no healthy social life, no home influences, no recognized position in religious and political communities. He can be nothing but a comet among the fixed stars and regularly revolving systems of the world, making a great show for the rather nebulous head which he carries, occupying more blue sky for a brief period than belongs to him, and then passing out of sight and out of memory, leaving no track.

I might go further, and show how nearly impossible it is for a public singer, who sings everything everywhere, who wanders over the world and lives upon the breath of popular applause, whose life seems almost necessarily made up of intrigues and jealousies, to be a religious man. No matter what the stage of the theatre or the platform of the concert room might be, or may have been; we know that now they are not the places where piety toward God is in such a state of high cultivation that good people throng before them for religious motive and inspiration. The whole atmosphere of a public singer's life is sensuous. Like the beggarly old reprobate in Rome who obtained a living by sitting to artists for his "religious expression," they coin their

Te Deums into dollars, and regard a mass as only a style of music to be treated in a professional way for other people who have sufficient interest in it to pay for the service. Man is a weak creature, and it takes a great many influences to keep him in the path of religious duty, and preserve his sympathy with those grand spiritual truths which relate to his noblest development and his highest destiny. These influences are not to be secured by a roving life, and constantly shifting society, and ministering to the tastes and seeking the favor of the vulgar crowd.

On the whole, Mr. Felix Mendelssohn Jones, I do not wonder that you are no better than you are. You have really had more influences operating against you than I had considered when I began to write this letter to you. Nevertheless, you ought to be ashamed of yourself and institute a reform. Recast you life. If you cannot settle down permanently in your profession in some town large enough to support you, and become a decent husband to your wife and father to your children, and take upon your shoulders your portion of the burdens of organized society, why, quit your profession, and go into some other business. I know you furnish a very slender basis for building a man upon, but you can at least cease to be a nuisance.

I know a good many musical men and women whom music or devotion to music has not damaged; but these men and women have entered as permanent elements into the society in which they live, and are something more than musicians. Singing is the most charming of all accomplishments when it is the voice of a noble nature and a generous culture; and all music, when it preserves its legitimate relations to the great interests of human society, is refining and liberalizing in its influence. But when music monopolizes the mind of a man; when it becomes the vehicle through which he ministers to his personal vanity; when it either becomes degraded to be the instrument for procuring his bread, or elevated to the position of a master passion, it spoils him. I pray that no friend or child of mine may become professionally a singing man or singing woman. All the circumstances that cluster about such a life, all the influences associated with it, and the great majority of its natural tendencies are against the development and preservation of a Christian style of life and character, and, consequently, against the best form of happiness here and the only form hereafter.

THE FOURTH LETTER.

To Hans Sachs Jones, Shoemaker.

CONCERNING HIS HABIT OF BUSINESS LYING.

YOU have always seemed to me to be an anomalous sort of personage. On the street, you are a respectable and decent man. I would take your note for any sum you would be likely to borrow, and rely upon its payment at maturity. Nay, I would accept your word of honor at any time, when your coat is on and the wax is off your fingers, with entire confidence. You have been intrusted with responsibilities in civil and social affairs, and have never betrayed them. You are a good husband, father, friend, and citizen, but you stand behind your counter from morning until night, and lie as continuously and coolly as if you were a flowing fountain of falsehood. You will not assail me in the street because I so plainly tell you this, for you know it is true, and that I like you too well to insult you. You know that you never made a pair of boots for me that did not cost you more lies than they cost me dollars.

I have stood before you, on some occasions, thoroughly astonished at the facility and ingenuity and boldness with which you lied your way out from among the fragments of your broken engagements. The glibness of your tongue, and the candor of your tone, and the immovable sincerity of your features, and the half-discouraged, half-wounded expression of face and voice with which you apologized for your failure to keep your pledges, were really overwhelming. I have sometimes wondered whether you did not suppose you were telling the truth—whether you had not, by some odd hallucination, come to believe that the causes of your failure to keep your pledges had a real and permanent existence. Never was so much sickness suffered by journeymen shoemakers as by yours. Never had shoemakers such sickly children, and never had shoemakers so many children born to them. It is a strange fatality, too, that always keeps your best workmen on a spree. I have never known any class of artisans drink so much as those you employ. You are always getting out of the right kind of leather at the wrong time, or suffering by some occurrence that renders it impossible for you to keep your promise and, at the same time, make just such a pair of boots or shoes as you feel particular about making for your particular customers. You resort to the most transparent flattery to keep your patrons good-natured, but there is not a man or woman who enters your shop who believes a word you utter. Day after day, and week after week, your promises are broken with regard to a single job, and your patrons smile in your face at the excuses which your tongue holds ready at all times; and you know that they know you are lying.

You are not a sinner in this respect above all shoemakers, and shoemakers are not sinners in this respect above all artisans and tradesmen. You happen to be a very perfect specimen of a class of men who work for the public in the performance of essential every-day jobs in the various mechanical arts. They do not all lie as much as you do, but many of them lie in the same way, and for the same reason. They are not all as cool about it as you are, and most of them are much less fertile and skilful than you are, but lying is their daily resort.

Now, what is there in your business, or in the relations to society of that class of employments to which yours belongs, to develop the untruthfulness which all must admit attaches to it in some degree? In the first place, you began business in a very small way, and were able to keep your promises, never making any that you did not intend to keep. Business increased, and you found among your best customers—those whose patronage you most desired to retain—a degree of unreasonable impatience which you could not withstand. You were imperiously urged into the making of pledges for the delivery of work which you could not make, consistently with your previously existing engagements. You were desirous to please; strong wills, backed by money, were brought to bear upon you; the keeping of your promise looked possible, even if not altogether practicable; and you promised. You felt, however, that somebody was to be disappointed, and you undertook to find an excuse which would lift the burden of blame from your own shoulders. You did not dare to stand before your customer a voluntary delinquent; so, when he came, and you were not ready to see him, you justified yourself by throwing the blame upon others, or upon circumstances over which you had no control. He may have believed you at first, but his faith in you soon wore out.

You learned, at length, that people loved to have their work promised early, and that they would take your apologies for failure goodnaturedly; and you ran into the habit of promising work early, with the expectation, if not the direct intention, to break your promise. I have given you jobs when I knew you lied while taking them, and expected to lie a great many times before you finished them. You have told me repeatedly that work was nearly finished when I knew it had not been begun; and all this for the purpose of pleasing me, and saving yourself from blame. You were not naturally untruthful, and you are not untruthful now where your business is not concerned, but in your business you have made falsehood the rule of your daily life. Your promises are always in advance of your power to perform, and the breaking of them has become habitual.

It is painful to see a man—otherwise so respectable—unreliable in the place where men meet him most; for it weakens his hold upon the popular regard, and cannot fail to depreciate his own self-respect. You must feel ashamed, at times, to realize that your word is not believed, and to know that you have not a customer in the world who feels at all sure about getting work done by you until it really is done and in his hands. The kind of life you lead must also be an exceedingly uncomfortable one. Now, my friend, there is not the slightest necessity for this, and there is no apology for it. It had a very natural beginning, but you ought to have learned long ago that it was not requisite either to your prosperity or your comfort. You get your work in spite of your lying, and not in consequence of it. That is the only thing people have against you. They give you their custom because you are a good workman, and for nothing else; and no man leaves your shop for another except for the reason that he cannot depend upon your word. You never made a dollar or saved a friend by all the lies you have told. Honesty, reliableness, truthfulness—these are at a premium in all the markets of the world; and you have made yourself miserable and contemptible throughout your life for nothing. Your business is always at loose ends, everybody is crowding you, many of them abuse you, and it all comes of your promising to do work before it is possible for you to do it. Not a decent man, whose custom is worth keeping, enters your shop who would not wait your time patiently, if he could rely upon having his job upon the day promised.

I have no doubt that, as you read this letter, you say to yourself that I talk as if a man *could* always keep promises, honestly made, and as if there were men in the world who never break promises. I know, indeed, that there is no man who can so thoroughly depend upon circumstances, or so control them, as always to be sure to keep his pledges. Sickness happens to all. Calamity in some form comes to all. Drunkenness sometimes overtakes a journeyman shoemaker, though, to tell the truth, such men are not commonly employed by masters who care about keeping their word. Men of business punctilio, and regular business habits, can always secure the best workmen. It is only the unreliable masters who are obliged to accept unreliable hands, though I would by no means intimate that I believe in your representations concerning the drunkenness of your workmen. Your men are shamefully belied; and if they knew how you slander them they would rebel. No, I admit that the most prompt and punctual men must fail, through unforeseen impediments, to keep all their promises; but such men do not lie their way out of their difficulty, and are only the more careful about making and keeping their engagements afterward.

To me, one of the most admirable things in the world is business punctilio. I think it is rare to find very bad men among thorough business men. I do not mean to say that a good business man is necessarily religious, or even necessarily without vices. I mean, simply, that it is difficult to be strictly honest in business, and sensitive in all matters pertaining to business engagements, and thoroughly punctual in the fulfilment of all business obligations, and at the same time to be loose in morals and dissipated in personal habits. I have great respect for those rigid laws of the counting room which regulate the dealings between man and man, and which make the counting room as exact in all matters of time and exchange as a banking house —which ignore friendship, affection, and all personal considerations whatsoever—which place neighbors and brothers on the same platform with enemies and aliens, and which make an autocrat of an accountant, who is, at the same time, strictly an obedient subject of his own laws. I say it is hard for a man to enter as a perfectly harmonious element into this grand system of business, and submit himself to its rigid rules, and maintain his position in it with perfect integrity, and, at the same time, be a very bad man. To a certain extent, he bows to and obeys a high standard of life. He may not always recognize fully the moral element which it embodies. He may take a selfish view of the whole matter; but he cannot be entirely insensible to the principle of personal honor which it involves, or fail to be influenced by the personal habits which it enforces. Some of the best business men I have ever known, have been the most charitable men I have ever known. Men who have acquired wealth by rigid adherence to business integrity, and who have sometimes been deemed harsh and hard by those with whom they have had business relations, have shown a liberality and a generosity toward objects of charity which have placed them among the world's benefactors. Men who have exacted the last fraction of a cent with one hand, in the way of business, have disbursed thousands of dollars with the other, in the way of charity.

On another side of this subject, it may be stated that it is not possible for a man to be careless in business affairs, or unmindful of his business obligations, without being weak or rotten in his personal character. Show me a man who never pays his notes when they are due, and who shuns the payment of his bills when it is possible, and does both these things as a habit, and I shall see a man whose moral character is, beyond all question, bad. We have had illustrious examples of this lack of business exactness. We have had great men who were in the habit of borrowing money without repaying it, or apologizing for not repaying it. We have had great men whose business habits were simply scandalous—who never paid a bill unless urged and worried, and who expended for their personal gratification every cent of money they could lay their hands upon. These delinquencies have been apologized for as among the eccentricities of genius, or as that unmindfulness of small affairs which naturally attends all greatness of intellect and intellectual effort; but the world has been too easy with them, altogether. I could name great men—and the names of some of them arise before the readers of this letter—who were atrociously dishonest. I do not care how great these men were. I do not care how many amiable and admirable traits they possessed. They were dishonest and untrustworthy men in their business relations, and that simple fact condemns them. I am ready to believe anything bad of a man who habitually neglects to fulfil his business obligations. Such a man is certainly rotten at heart. He is not to be trusted with a public responsibility, or a rum bottle, or a woman.

Now, Mr. Hans Sachs Jones, you have customers of this class. Will you permit me to ask you how you like them? Some of these men are poor, but quite as many of them are rich. You lied to them a great many times before they made their little bills with you, and they have lied to you a great many times since. When you have had money to raise, they have promised to furnish it to you, and then they have failed to keep their pledges. Not unfrequently, when you have upbraided them for disappointing you, they have retorted by telling you that you made them wait for their work, and that it is perfectly proper that you should wait for your pay. Their reply was a fair one, so far as you were concerned. It was just as much a matter of business honor that you should keep your promises, as it was that they should keep theirs. It was just as wrong for you to promise your work before you could give it to them, as it was for your customers to promise to pay you before they could pay you, or before they intended to pay you. In your heart, you think these men are very mean, and in their hearts they think that you are just as mean as they are, and they are right. Their plea leaves you defenceless, and they banter and badger you until you become disgusted with your business and yourself. Oh! if you had never given these customers of yours an advantage over you, by your constant failures to keep your word with them, you would be worth a good many more dollars to-day than you are.

Then you should remember that you owe a debt of honor to your guild. A very admirable thing among tradesmen of the same class is that *esprit de corps* which enables them to join hands in a recognized community of honor and of interest, and to look upon their trade as the kind mother that feeds them and that deserves at their hands the treatment due from grateful and chivalrous sons. You have doubtless heard of associations of men engaged in much humbler employments than yours (humbler in the world's judgment), that really won the respect and admiration of the communities in which they lived—men who felt strengthened and ennobled by their association—men who came by their association to feel the slightest insult offered to their trade as a personal affront. I say that this *esprit de corps* is a very admirable thing, and, further, that it gives, or may give, a true dignity to any honest calling under heaven. We do not have so much of this in this country as we ought to have. All European countries are ahead of us in this matter, principally, perhaps, for the reason that in those countries the acquisition and pursuit of trades are more particularly a matter of legal regulation. Here a man may set up a trade whether he ever learned it or not, and few learn their trades thoroughly. It is more difficult, therefore, to secure community of feeling among those engaged in the same pursuits here than abroad; but it is none the less desirable and necessary, that, among good workmen like yourself, there should be brotherhood of feeling and interest—pride and sympathy of guild. It would give you dignity, protection, respectability; and you would feel in all your business transactions that, however reckless you might be of disgrace to yourself, you have no right to disgrace your business, or your brotherhood.

I repeat, then, that you owe a debt of honor to your guild. There are many men engaged in the same calling with you who scorn the petty arts of falsehood to which you resort. They are men of character—men who never make a promise which they do not intend to keep, and who faithfully and conscientiously strive to keep every promise which they make. These are the men who give to your calling all the respectability which it possesses. All labor of the hands, pursued for bread, is honorable, and honorable alike. One trade is respectable above another only in consequence of the superior respectability of the class of men engaging in it. Now you have a right, in a certain sense, to disgrace yourself; but you have no right to disgrace your trade and your guild. Your devotion to this idea should be almost religious; for, in a certain degree, you have the reputation of the whole class with which you are identified in interest in your keeping, and you are bound by every principle of justice and honor not to betray it.

I have not appealed, in what I have said to you on this subject, to those higher motives of conduct which grow out of your relations to the God of truth, nor do I propose to. You know, just as well as I do, that your system of business lying is morally wrong. I simply wish, in closing this letter, to call your attention to the fact that you have arrived at the point where your conscience ceases to trouble you. You do not use profane language. You are shocked when you hear others use it, but you are aware that many of your acquaintances swear from habit, and, by habitual swearing, have ceased to look upon their profanity as profanity. They take the names of God and Jesus Christ in vain, and call for curses upon the heads even of their friends, without a thought of sin, and without a twinge of conscience. Over a certain region of their moral sense profanity has trampled, until it has trampled the life all out of it. So, over a certain region of your moral sense, these lies of yours have trod their daily course, until not a blade of grass or a flower is left to give token of life, or breathe complaint of the invaders. They have trampled out all sensibility, and you lie without feeling it; and when you are detected and indignantly rebuked, as you sometimes are, you only feel your detection as an inconvenience, which might have been avoided by more ingenious lying. I beg you to discontinue this ruinous practice, and see if sensibility will not once more inform those functions of your moral nature which persistent abuse has indurated and rendered useless.

THE FIFTH LETTER.

To Edward Payson Jones.

CONCERNING HIS FAILURE TO YIELD TO HIS CONVICTIONS OF DUTY.

AS I write your name, there comes before me the vision of a fair-haired, blue-eyed boy, who had been fed by smiles and pleasant words at home so constantly that his whole nature had been sweetened by them. I remember how you used to look up into my face for recognition and for the greeting and the smile which you had learned to crave and to expect of everybody. Into few faces did those expectant blue eyes look in vain, for you were a universal favorite. I remember that I was always so much impressed by your pure and precious nature that I could never resist the impulse to put my arm around you, and draw you to my heart. It was easy to love you, and sweet to be loved by you; and those who knew your sainted mother knew why you were what you were in personal and spiritual loveliness. That mother has been dead a long time, but do you not sometimes recall her reason for giving you the name of Edward Payson? Ah, yes! I know that you must sometimes remember that in her heart of hearts—even before you were born—she dedicated you to the service of the Saviour of men, and that she crowned you with a name hallowed by a wide wealth of Christian associations, that she might be reminded of her gift whenever she pronounced it. The absorbing hope of her life was to see you in the pulpit, and to hear you preach the everlasting gospel. To compass this end, she would have been willing to work her fingers to the bone; to live in want; to deny to herself every worldly pleasure; nay, to lay down her life itself. She died, as you know, without seeing the attainment of the object for which she had labored and prayed so ardently.

Well, you are a man; and you are just as widely a favorite to-day as you were when you were a boy; but you are not the man whom your mother prayed you might become, and are not likely to be. That you are stifling convictions of duty by the course which you are pursuing every man knows who remembers your early training and the nature upon which that training could not fail to leave its impress. You are a man whom everybody loves—whom everybody praises—whom everybody believes to be in a measure the subject of Christian conviction—whom everybody believes to be, within certain limits, controlled by Christian principle; yet, in an irreligious community, you have never, in a manly way, declared yourself in the possession and on the side of personal Christianity. Under these circumstances, there are some things which it seems to me to be my duty to say to you. Will you read them?

Christianity is everything, or it is nothing—it is divine, or it is nothing—it has a right to the entire control of your life, or it has no claims at all. Is it necessary that I should argue to you the transcendent worth, the divine origin, or the grand claims of that religion which made an angel of your mother, and transformed the little room in which she died into heaven's gateway? Is it necessary for me to assure you that these convictions of duty which haunt you everywhere, which assert themselves in your heart in every scene of questionable mirth and careless society, are not superstitions engendered by early education in error? Is it necessary that I should try to prove to you that a life which does not acknowledge a rule of action imposed by the Author of life must necessarily be a life of transgression and the fruits of transgression? Not at all. You do not ask me to do this. You know—you are entirely convinced—that you owe the devoted allegiance of your heart, the obedience of your will, and the gift of your life to that religion in which alone abides the secret of the purification and salvation of yourself and your race. You are convinced that, without Christianity, this world would be as dark as the infernal shades—that it alone gives significance to life—that it alone can give such direction to its issues that they shall rise to everlasting harmony and everlasting happiness.

There are those around you who do not believe in these things. They were not trained as you were trained. Their mother was not your mother, and they were not endowed with your nature. They do not possess your pureness of insight. In short, they are not, to any great extent, the subjects of religious conviction; and yet you choose these men for your associates and fellows. I ask you now whether you consider it a manly thing for one like you, with your convictions, to live like one who has no convictions—whether you do not feel that you are really disgracing yourself and depreciating your own self-respect by constantly refusing to yield your heart and life to the claim of those convictions which never leave you.

While you give such answers to these questions as I know you cannot fail to give, and while you half resolve to yield to convictions which I know are pressing upon you now with redoubled force, you look forward to the possible consequences of a change in the motives and regulating forces of your life. Before your imagination, glaring gloomily in the distance, there stands a lion in the way. A hearty and unconditional surrender to your convictions would involve changes in your social relations, in habits which have become endeared to you, in the general sources from which you have drawn the satisfactions of your life. You know that a change like this would bring with it a public declaration of your faith, and a publicly formed union with those men and women who have organized themselves into the Christian church. You shrink from this with a sensitiveness of selfish pride which ought to show you that you are very much farther from being a Christian than you suppose yourself to be, for, with all your consciousness of religious convictions stifled, you are fondly cherishing the fancy that you are already quite as good as Christians average.

Now you know, my friend, that I do not entertain a very extravagent opinion of the prerogatives of the Christian church. No church has the power to save you or me, or to say whether you or I shall be saved or not. You know also that I am no propagandist of sectarian doctrines and policies. If a church is a

Christian church, that is enough. I do not care the value of a straw by what name it calls itself. I look upon it as a school of Christian disciples—of imperfect men and women who have chosen Christianity as their religion—their reforming motive and their rule of life—the grand system of spiritual truths in which they have garnered their hopes for this life and the life to come—garnered their temporal and eternal satisfactions. I do not believe in the infallibility of any church, or in the sinlessness of any member of a church. Nay, I do not believe that the act of uniting with a church has in itself any saving grace whatever. Church is not Christianity, and Christianity is not church, in any practical sense. A man is probably just as good a Christian the moment before joining a church as he is the moment after; but a Christian will cast in his lot with Christians, if he possesses a decent degree of manhood, and share with them in the Christian work of the world.

I know very well what the influences are which restrain you from yielding to your convictions, and from taking the public step which would naturally follow such a surrender. You love praise. You love to be loved by everybody, and you have very strong friends among all sorts of people. The good people praise you, and feel as if you, with your straightforward life and pure habits, belonged to them. The bad people love you, and feel that, by your practical denial of the claims of Christianity, you make their position respectable. But where do you find your delights? Who are your cronies? Whose society do you seek? When you feel inclined to yield to your convictions of duty, whose are the shrugging shoulders and the pitying smiles—whose are the quiet jest and the banter and badinage which come in quick vision to you, to shame and scare you? My friend, you do not love that which is characteristically Christian society. You love that which has no Christian element in it except the element of decency; and you feel that to become the member of a Christian church would throw you out of sympathy with men whose good will and good fellowship you count among your choicest treasures. You cannot bear that these men should think you weak and womanish. You cannot bear to become the subject of their lenient and charitable scorn.

Human friendship is very sweet. These ties that bind heart to heart—these sympathetic responses of kindred natures—these loves among men glorify human life; but they not unfrequently form a bond of union so strong that one powerful nature will, through their aid, carry whithersoever it will—even into the jaws of destruction—all the lives that are joined with it. The ice upon the mountain side links rock to rock till the lightning or the earthquake loosens the hold of the giant of the group, and it drags them all into the valley below. Life nearly always follows the current of its friendships or flows parallel with it. If a man finds his most grateful companionships among those who are irreligious—either negatively or positively—he shows just what and where his heart is. Like seeks and sympathizes with like.

I ask you, Edward Payson Jones, to apply this test to yourself. What kind of society do you delight in most? Do you love and cling to those most who best represent to you the religion in which your mother lived and died, or those who practically hold that religion in very light esteem? I ask you to apply this test, because I think you are entertaining the idea that, although you make no professions, you are quite as good a Christian as those are who do. My friend, you choose freely to give your most intimate friendships to the worldlings by whom you are surrounded. I state the fact, and leave you to your own conclusions.

There is another powerful influence which dissuades you from yielding to your convictions. You are absorbed in business. All the activities of your nature are given to it. Great business responsibilities are upon you, and your heart gives them glad entertainment, for they are full of promise to your ambition and your desire for wealth. Business occupies nearly all your waking thoughts, and even haunts your pillow and breaks your slumbers. It obtrudes itself upon your family life, and monopolizes both your time and your vital power. Your heart is so full that you have no room in it for another object. Wife and children and friends and business—these four; but the greatest of these, practically, is business. If you will candidly examine yourself, you will see that I do not overrate this power of business which shuts out from your heart a guest who sits and shivers in its anteroom in the cold society of your convictions. To make this matter still worse, you are thrown into contact with men in the way of business upon whom you are, to a certain extent, dependent for your prosperity, who hold Christianity and its professed friends and possessors in contempt. You cannot bear this contempt. These men, with their business thoughts and schemes, break in upon your Sabbaths, they tempt you, they familiarize your ears with profanity, and invest you constantly with an atmosphere of worldliness. You have in your present position no defence against the influence of these associations. You have never declared yourself upon the side of Christianity, and these business friends of yours know it. They recognize you as one of their own number, and treat you accordingly; and yet, you are foolish enough to believe, or to try to make yourself believe, that a man can be just as good a Christian outside of the church as inside of it! Why, my friend, you are a man of honor. However much disgusted and abused, your nature is a chivalrous one. If you felt yourself identified with a great cause, would you betray it? Have you not often comforted yourself with the consideration that, if you have failed to become what your convictions have urged you to become, no one has been harmed but yourself?

I have spoken of you as a man of honor. I think you are sensitively such. I know of no man who more thoroughly despises a mean and unmanly spirit, or a mean and unmanly deed. If you were to see a man who, for any reason, should cast his vote at an election contrary to his convictions of political duty, or any man who should stand upon the fence in an important canvass and refuse to place himself on the side of the right, or who, in a great public emergency, should fail to perform his duty through absorbing devotion to his private pursuits, you would think him a mean man. You would despise particularly one whom you knew to be the subject of strong political convictions, which were so feebly pronounced that all parties claimed him. I take your own standard and apply it to you. I say, on the authority of your own best judgments, that it is mean and unmanly for you, with your strong religious convictions, to refuse to stand by them, and act up to them. It is mean and unmanly for you to refuse to identify yourself with the society, and assist in maintaining and forwarding the cause of those whom, sooner or later, you deliberately intend to join, and whom you feel and know to be in the right. If you were not convinced of the truth, I should be more charitable toward you. If there remained anything to be done in shaping the judgment of your intellect and your heart, you would have some excuse; but no such exigency exists. No, sir: you are convinced; but you flinch, and you refuse to stand in a manly way by what you know and feel to be right.

While I thus blame you, I pity you. I know how much your heart bends before these words of mine, and how impotent you feel for action in the right direction. You almost feel as if your hands and feet were tied. You almost feel as if you *must* follow your old friendships—that they have fastened themselves to you by hooks of steel which cannot be broken. You feel that your business is upon you, and all its associations, and that neither can be lifted. You feel that you really have no room in your life for those experiences and those duties which accompany the surrender of the heart to religion. You feel yourself walled around by obstacles, and, what is really worse than this, you know that you grow more and more in love with the life you lead, and less inclined to take the direction of your early training. The oath does not shock you as it once did; vulgarity is not as offensive as it once was; you have learned to look more leniently upon the vices of the men by whom you are surrounded; worldliness does not seem so barren a form of life as formerly; you are charmed and excited by success; and you cannot deny to yourself the fact that, strong as your convictions of duty are, your heart and your life are growing more and more widely estranged from them. Where do you suppose all this will end? You have common sense, and can judge as well as I. Do habits grow weaker by long continuance? Are the cares of business less absorbing as life advances? Is moral conviction the stronger for constant denial and insult? I say, you have common sense, and can judge as well as I. You know as well as I that this life of yours must have a rupture with its surroundings—that your feet must turn into another path—that you must yield yourself a conquest to your convictions, or that your life will be one of disaster, and that its end will be wretchedness or an induration worse than wretchedness.

You are surrounded by a crowd of men and women who do not regard life as a very serious thing. They take it carelessly and gayly. You see the multitudes rushing along in the pursuit of baubles. Men live and die, and there comes back no voice to tell whether they sleep with the brutes or wake with the angels. Men eat and sleep, and love and hate, and make display of their equipage, and pursue their ambitions and indulge in all the forms of vanity and pride, and all life comes at last to seem like a sort of phantasmagoria—empty, unreal, insignificant. You see that these convictions of yours have no place in the multitude of minds around you, and no place in the current of life by which you feel yourself borne along. There are moments, I suppose, when you doubt the soundness of these convictions—when you half believe that you are the victim of a morbid conscience, or of a superstitious impression. At such moments as these—when the tricks of the world delude you most, come back to your mother, and learn the truth. That life of hers, so pure and unselfish and useful, and that death of hers, so peaceful and triumphant, are realities. They can never lie to you, and the moment you touch them, you know that you touch something divine—something by the side of which all worldliness and wealth and material success are chaff.

You will perceive, in what I have written to you, that I have not undertaken to convince you of anything. I have not undertaken even to deepen your convictions. I have simply endeavored to reveal you and your own experience to yourself, and to urge you to yield to convictions which I know are striving to gain the control of your life. I have simply urged you to be true to yourself—to take a bold, manly, consistent stand upon the side which you know to be right—to be a Christian man in Christian society, and to refuse longer to stand upon what you mistakenly regard as neutral ground. Do you know that you are abusing and ruining yourself? Do you realize that the passage of every day renders it less probable that your convictions will ever gain the victory over you?

I appreciate the struggle it would cost you to welcome the new motive and change the policy and issues of your life. The preacher may talk as he will of the ease of the path of life and the ease of yielding up the will, but you and I know that there is no ease about it. We know that whatever may be the truth touching the doctrine of universal total depravity, it is not *natural* for *us* to lead religious lives. It takes sacrifice and fighting and heroism to do that. I know it, and you know it. Easy to be a Christian man? It is mean for a man like you not to be one—it is wrong for a man like you not to be one—but Heaven knows it is not easy for you to be one, or you would have been one long ago. No, my friend; it will be hard for you to be one, and it will grow harder every year till you become one. But it pays, and when you are once fairly on the right side, you will not care for the struggle, for you will have good company, a clean conscience, and an outlook into the far future unclouded and full of inspiration.

THE SIXTH LETTER.

To Mrs. Jessy Bell Jones.

CONCERNING THE DIFFICULTY SHE EXPERIENCES IN KEEPING HER SERVANTS.

IT has been stated to me, confidentially, that you have had nineteen different cooks and thirteen chambermaids in your house during the past year. This may be slightly above the annual average. I should hope so. I do not understand how flesh and blood could endure such changes. Yet you live and thrive; and the new servants come and go at about the usual number per month. Your husband grew tired, long ago, with rasping against so much new domestic material, but has learned fortitude by practice. One or two attempts on his part to tell you that there were women who kept their servants for months and years without change, and to convince you that it was possible that there were bad mistresses in the world as well as bad servants, resulted in scenes which will be avoided in future. Not if he were to see a procession of young women entering your house and emerging from it through all the weary year—not if he were to hear a constant storm raging in the kitchen and echoing throughout the passages and chambers, would he ever intimate that you were not the paragon of mistresses, and that your girls were not the meanest, dirtiest, sauciest pot-slewers that ever invaded an abode of civilization.

No, Mrs. Jones; you will have it all your own way, without any interference from him. He knows you are in the wrong, and so do you; but he will never tell you so again. On the contrary, he will sympathize with you after a fashion, and take your part in all your quarrels and all your domestic difficulties; but he will quietly wish, meanwhile, that you had the faculty of getting along pleasantly with your servants. I have intimated to you that you know yourself to be in the wrong. You are not a fool. On the contrary, you are a very sharp, bright woman, and you cannot fail to see that there is a reason, *somewhere in your house*, for your failure to keep your servants. Your neighbor lives in the same climate that you do. The roof of her house is covered by slate from the same quarry; her Stuart's stove is of the same size as yours; her laundry is no more convenient than yours; her servants are no better fed than yours; she gives no better wages than you; but she keeps her servants, and you do not keep yours. When one of her servants marries, or sickens, or, for any reason, wishes to leave her, fifty others stand ready to take her place, and she has her pick of them all, while you are obliged to take such as come, and such as feel compelled to come after having heard that you are a hard mistress. For you must know that masters and mistresses have reputations among servants—reputations made up, and weighed, and widely known. You, and a hundred other women whom I know, have bad reputations among servants; and when you deal with them you are always obliged to deal with them under the disadvantage which a bad reputation bears with it.

Suppose we have a little plain talk about these matters, and see if we can get at an understanding of them. You will pardon me if I tell you, in the first place, that you are an opinionated person, which is a mild way of stating that, in certain respects, you are very conceited. Your pet conceit is that you are a model housekeeper, and your opinion is that you know the best and only proper modes of doing the work in your kitchen, and in your house generally. You have your own way of doing everything. You have your particular order, in which all things about you are to be done. The machinery of your household arrangements, as it exists in your mind, is a perfect whole, and every executive element that you introduce into it must adapt itself to that machinery, or it is cast out at once, or is so harassed that it casts itself out. Suppose a girl enters your kitchen who understands her business, but who has learned it under another mistress, and a different household economy. She has learned to do her work in a certain way, and after a certan order. She has her notions as well as you. It is quite possible that those notions may be in many respects better than yours. You insist, however, from the moment she enters your service, that she shall do your work in your way. You do not wait to see results. You do not wait to see how she will succeed if left entirely to herself, but you go into the kitchen with her, and superintend every act. You give her no freedom, you encourage no independent effort; you take the whole burden on yourself, and insist that she shall be your machine. When she forgets your directions, or steps aside from them, you find fault with her. She soon tires with this sort of treatment, and you are told to look for another girl.

I have told you that your pet conceit is that you are a model housekeeper, and tried to show that your difficulties with your servants grow out of your insisting that they shall do everything in your way. I think I may justly say, in addition, that there is a certain sensitiveness of will in your constitution which aggravates these difficulties. You are imperious. There is one spot in the world where you have the right to rule—one spot where that will of yours has the right to assert itself and make itself law. Perhaps there is no other spot where your will is recognized. Your house is your only domain. There you are a queen, and you are sensitively alive to all interference with your prerogatives. It frets you to feel that there is any other person in the house, with a will, who has anything to do or say about your domestic affairs. You do not feel that a servant has a right to an independent opinion on any subject connected with her service; and when any such opinion finds practical expression, it enrages you. A servant may feel that if she does her work well, in the way most convenient to her, she does all that you can reasonably claim; but you feel that unless that work—in all its modes and particulars—has followed the channel of your will, you have been insulted in your own house. In short, madam, you are "touchy," and when you are touched, you scold, and when you scold, off goes your girl. You have excellent pluck, however. I have never known you to lament the loss of a servant. They were always such terrible creatures that you were glad to get rid of them.

I do not know how you came to be just the sort of

mistress you are. You were a very pleasant little girl, with a sweet temper. It has really puzzled me to find out the reason for your peculiar development. I suppose there must be an "ugly streak" in you somewhere, but you did not show it when you were a child. Your hair is red, I know (call it golden), and your eyes black, but the hair is beautiful and soft, and the eye has a world of love in it for the man it worships and for his children. My theory is that every nature which has any force in it will assert itself somewhere, in some form, and that if it fails to be recognized in society, it will make itself recognized where there are none to dispute its claims. I do not recall a single famous housekeeper, with a splendid faculty for getting rid of servants, and a bad reputation among them, who, at the same time, was a woman widely recognized in society. If you, Mrs. Jessy Bell Jones, were an acknowledged power and authority in the social circle; if you were a fine musician with the opportunity to charm your friends; if you had a high degree of literary culture and were received everywhere in literary circles as an ornament or an equal; if you possesed a recognized value out of your house, or in your parlor, beyond other women of your class or set, I think you would be content—that your servants would get along well enough, and that you would get along well enough with them.

But you have turned housekeeper, and directed all your energies and all your ambitions, and all your will, into the channel of housekeeping; and woe to the servant who stands in your way.

Under these circumstances, there are a few practical questions which it would be well for you to ask yourself. Do you feel that your system of management pays? Do you enjoy these constant troubles with your servants? Do you think your husband enjoys them, and your irate or plaintive representations of them? Do you not feel sometimes as if you would be willing to give a good deal of money, and put yourself to a good deal of trouble to get along as smoothly with your girls as some of your neighbors do? Do you wish or expect always to live the same sort of life you are living now?

In making up your answers to these questions, you must remember that any change which may be made must begin with yourself. If you are really willing to make sacrifices for the sake of peace and perpetuity in your domestic arrangements, you can have both; but you will be obliged to sacrifice your will, and a good many of your pet notions concerning housekeeping. If it is sweeter to you to have your will, than it is to keep girls steadily who will serve you reasonably well, why, of course, that settles the question; though it is doubtful whether you would get so much of your will accomplished by sending them away as you would by keeping them.

You must take certain facts into consideration when you hire a servant. The most important is, perhaps, that when you hire a servant you do not buy a slave. You do not buy the right to badger and scold her, to impose upon her unreasonable burdens, or to treat her as if she were only an animal. You are to remember, also, that there are two sides to this relation of mistress and servant. Labor is not a drug in this country yet, thank Heaven, and it is quite as important to you that you have servants, as it is to your girls that they do service. You and your girls are under mutual obligations to treat each other well. In England and on the Continent, where human life, owing to peculiar circumstances, is in excess—a condition which cannot possibly exist in healthily constituted society—servants are born into families often, and grow up dependants, forever attached to the family name and interest. A good place and a permanent one is equivalent to a treasure with them, and they will make many sacrifices to preserve it, Here, it is different. Labor is everywhere in demand, and no girl ever steps out of your door without knowing that, within a short space of time, she can easily find another place, with a chance at least for better treatment than you give her.

There is another consideration to which I am sure sufficient importance has not been attached. You are a Protestant, as the majority of Americans are, and you know that servants who come to you, and whom the most of us employ, are Catholics. It is notorious and incontrovertible that your servants are taught to consider you a heretic—a person who has no religion, and who is bound as directly for hell as if she were a murderess. It is cruel to teach these ignorant women such horrible stuff, but they are taught it. The Irish girl in your kitchen, who perhaps does not know her alphabet—who probably has not the first idea of the vital truths of Christianity—regards you and the whole community of American Protestants with contempt, as the accursed of God, and of those whom she supposes to be His representatives on the earth. She has been bred to this opinion, and it may be the only really strong opinion she has in her mind. She has no doubt that a drunken, profane, lying scoundrel, if he is only in the Catholic church, has a better chance for heaven than the purest Protestant that lives, because she has been taught from childhood that there is no salvation out of "the church." Now I say that women thus bred cannot possibly entertain such a degree of respect for you that they will take patiently your style of treatment. It is notorious that they receive, even with abject humility, indignities from masters and mistresses belonging to their church, while they exact from Protestants the last ounce of that which is their due as Christian women. I do not complain of this particularly, but I allude to it to show that you, and every Protestant mistress in America, must necessarily labor under disadvantages in the management of servants.

There is still another consideration which you and all other mistresses should make, which is, that all girls who are good for anything must do their work in their own way, or not do it well. One of the hardest things in this world for any person who has brains, and the power to use them, is to do another person's work is another person's way. To most persons, the attempt to do this is always disgusting, and often distressing. It is only hacks and blockheads that can possibly submit themselves to the degradation which such a service involves. You must always be content with these, or you must have servants who have some notions and ways of their own. A servant may be a very humble person, but she has her will, and her pride, and her desire to be somebody in her place, just as much as you have; and she will not sell her right to entertain an opinion and have her way in the little details of her service for a dollar and seventy-five cents a week, to you or anybody else. I must confess that I sympathize with her in this thing. Among your servants you may reasonably require results economically attained, but all that exactness which insists on dusting a piano from the north to the south, or prescribes the whole routine of a kitchen, to its minutest particular, and vigilantly maintains it, is an insult and a hardship, and is certain to be regarded and treated as such by every servant who is good for anything.

Now if you are willing to make all these considerations, you can have servants and keep them. If you are willing to consider that your servant is not a slave, and has a right to the treatment due to a rational woman, that you have no right to harass her with your notions or your petulancies, that you are under as strong an obligation to treat her well as she is to treat you well, that she has been bred to consider you a heretic—one for whom God has no respect and Heaven no home, that it is in the nature of things impossible for a really capable and good servant to do her work cheerfully and well when she is required to do it in a way not her own, that in this world of imperfection there are some things which will be unpleasant "in the best regulated families," that it is better to enjoy peace generally, than to have one's will in unimportant particulars,—I say that if you are willing to consider all these things, I do not see why you may not keep your servants as long as other people, and have just as good a time with them. It will be very hard for you to break into this thing, and I know of but one way for you to proceed. Get a new cook—the best you can find—and promise to pay her good wages. Then hold up your right hand and swear in the presence of your husband (who will record your oath with unaffected delight), that you will not enter your kitchen for a month, unless it be to praise some particular dish, or tell the cook how nicely everything looks in her domain. At the end of the month, you will have learned that cooking can be carried on in your family without your help, that your cook is contented and pleased, that you are happier than you have been for ten years, that you have more time for reading and dressing and visiting, and that the inconveniences attending a course like this are much less than those which have thus far accompanied your housekeeping life. I would not prescribe constant absence from the kitchen as the only safe course for all; I simply say that it is the only safe course for you. After a few months shall have passed away, and you shall have come to love your new way of life, it will be safe for you to take a general oversight of your kitchen again. You must run, however, whenever you feel the old fever coming on.

Did you ever think how easy it would be to make your pretty name—"Jessy Bell"—into Jezebel? It would be just as easy to transform your pretty nature into one which that name alone would fitly represent. I do not account you one of those women, possessed with the devil, who are as much the horror of husband and children as of servants. You are not even one of those women (from whom the gods defend me and mine!) to whom the vision of a speck of dirt is the cause of a convulsion and the inspiration of a lecture that would frighten anything but a clod out of the house. Mysterious are the ways of women. There be women who take delight in being miserable and making others so; who can scold, or cry, or howl, or spit fire; who would not be happy if they could be; who badger everybody—implacable, unreasonable, abominable women, from whom all gentle womanhood has departed. There be such women as these, I say, and you have seen them. Will you permit me to tell you that you are in great danger of becoming one of them? It is not hard for a woman in your circumstances, who has set up for model housekeeper, with a sensitive will and a determination to have everything in her own way, to neglect the cultivation of those goodnesses and graces which keep her spirit soft, and keep it in sympathy with those who love her.

The secret of living comfortably in this world, consists in making the best of such unpleasant things as cannot be avoided. It is necessary for you to have servants, and it is necessary for you to obtain your servants from the same class that the rest of us do. They are not a very reliable class of people, but they have in them the labor that you want, and must have. The question simply is, whether, under the circumstances, you will make yourself and your husband miserable by insisting on that which you have never yet succeeded in getting—perfect servants—the perfect slaves of your will—or whether you will get the best servants you can, make allowance for their shortcomings, and put up with their imperfect service for the sake of peace. The way in which you answer this question will determine everything concerning the comfort of your home life, and much concerning your own personal character. The best way for you is to confess—to yourself, at least—that you have been all in the wrong, and to change your entire policy. Turn your energies in some other direction. Be as good a housekeeper as you can, under the circumstances, and be content with such modest attainments as servants moderately intelligent and immoderately independent will permit. Thus will Mrs. Jessy Bell Jones live long and comfortably on the earth, rejoicing the hearts of her husband and children, enjoying a good reputation among the class on which she must depend for service, taking comfort in ladylike pursuits, and avoiding the imminent danger in which she stands of becoming "Mrs. Jezebel Jones."

THE SEVENTH LETTER.

To Salathiel Fogg Jones, Spiritualist.

CONCERNING THE FAITH AND PROSPECTS OF HIS SECT OF RELIGIONISTS.

YOU happen to be one of the men ordained from the foundation of the world to be a Spiritualist. There are many unlike you who are Spiritualists, but there are none like you who are not. You have all that natural love of what is novel and marvellous, and that peculiar mixture of credulity and skepticism, and that perverse disposition to run against the feelings and prejudices of people, which would lead you to embrace Spiritualism. Wherever I find a man who possesses your peculiar nature and character, I always find a Spiritualist; for if Spiritualism does not come to him, he goes to it. You were a Fourierite when I first knew you, and you rode the hobby of Fourierism until you rode it to death. Every "ism" that has been started during the last twenty years has numbered you among its champions. You were a zealous abolitionist until abolitionism became popular, and then, without turning against it, you seemed to lose your interest in it. When Spiritualism made its appearance, I knew that you would be a Spiritualist, as well as I knew that "fire, ascending, seeks the sun." It was the natural thing for you.

I was not at all surprised, therefore, when you caught me by the button-hole one day, at the corner of a street, and announced to me the conviction that you could demonstrate the immortality of the human soul. You may, perhaps, remember the smile which your announcement excited. I confess that it amused me. You seemed as interested and pleased about the matter as if you had never heard of such a thing as immortality before. A book had been in your hands ever since you could read, that told you all about it. A belief in this immortality had incorporated itself into the constitution and governments of all the powerful nations of the world; had moulded civilization—nay, had created civilization out of barbarism; had introduced into society its highest motives and its most purifying elements; had sustained the courage and inspired the hope of multitudes of dying saints and martyrs through all ages; had surrounded you all your life with the evidences of its vitality, and yet, you had but just satisfied yourself on the question, by means of unaccountable raps on a table, in the dark, which, through a little assistance of your own, had spelled out, in bad orthography and worse syntax, an insignificant sentence! Here was a moral force that had moved the world, yet it had not moved you! You—wiser, more acute, less credulous, less superstitious—had waited to see a table dance before you could believe in that realm of spiritual things which has hung above and embraced you since you were born, and which has always had a representative in your own bosom!

This has been one of the marvels of these latter-day developments in Spiritualism: that men who have been skeptical on all cognate subjects, and have resisted all the moral and spiritual evidences of immortality—resisted all the evidences germane to the subject—have bowed like bulrushes before the proofs that come to them from a mysteriously played banjo, or a common place message, pretended to be rapped out by a friend on the other side of the river. It took Materialism to prove Spiritualism to these very acute men; and they thought that, because they had seen matter moved by spirit, or what they supposed to be spirit, they had made a prodigious advance. They have been floored by proofs that do not add a hair's weight to the faith of any genuine Christian in the world. They think that they have made a discovery, and that Christians are afraid of it, when the truth is that they have made no discovery whatever, and that Christians are above it. The proofs of spirituality and of immortality, to be found in what is called Spiritualism, are the grossest that can possibly be produced, supposing them to be genuine. They are proofs that deal with matter exclusively, and appeal to the commonest and lowest order of minds. It is you, my friend, who are behind the age, and not the Christians at whose faith you scoff, simply because you are not up to it and cannot appreciate it. You receive a little thing because you are not sufficient to receive a large one.

I do not intend, in the few paragraphs which I propose to write to you, to undertake the overthrow of your proofs of Spiritualism. I am willing, indeed, to confess that I have witnessed, among much that was undoubtedly the result of deception and jugglery, phenomena which I could not rationally account for by any other theory than that which assigns to them a spiritual origin. But those phenomena have never contributed anything to my conviction that I am immortal, and that there is a realm of spiritual existence which holds the product of unnumbered worlds and the history of an eternity. They have never made so much as a ripple on the surface of my faith. Their apparent aim has been so limited, many of them have been so low and frivolous, some of them have been so vicious, and all have had so much more to do with matter than with spirit, or with spiritual truth, that they have never seemed worthy for an instant to have any consideration as parts of any religious system, or as opponents of any religious system. It is an insult to common sense, no less than an offence to decency, to compare the conglomerate trash which has been issued as the teachings of the spirits with Christianity, as a system of religion; and it is a simple impossibility for a true and hearty Christian to accept in the place of his faith the peepings and the mutterings of a pack of lying demons, whose deceptions and tricks are acknowledged by their best friends.

The rule which the Author of Christianity announced, and which the common judgment of the world has indorsed—that a tree is known by its fruits—is one which it is now proper to apply to Spiritualism. Fifteen years have passed since the new sect made its first batch of proselytes. It is time to be looking for the fruit of this tree, which, at the beginning, was declared to be so full of golden promise. I ask you if you have found Spiritualism particularly nourishing to yourself. Are you a better man than you were ten years ago? How much progress have you made toward real spirituality? How much more devout is your worship of the Great God than it was before you were convinced of the immortality of your own soul? How much have your affections been purified, your love of spiritual things strengthened, your lust for sensual indulgence diminished, by this new faith of yours? Has your sense of moral obligation grown stronger? Has your benevolence increased? Has your love of all that is good and pure grown brighter, while the sensual delights of your animal life have faded? These are important questions to you, and they are very important questions to Spiritualism itself.

I must be plain with you, and tell you that if Spiritualism has improved you I have failed to see it. I do not see that you have even made any progress intellectually. You pretend that Spiritualism reveals great truths in which abide the seeds of progress and perfection for a race, but these seeds do not germinate in you. On the contrary, you seem content to stand at the threshold of your new religion, and to amuse yourself with the same insignificant phenomena which first attracted your attention. I hear of your holding weekly, or semi-weekly, sessions or "circles" where there are the ringing of bells, and playing of guitars, and the scraping of fiddles, and the tipping of tables, and the rubbing of faces, and the rapping of knuckles. It is the same old story of a sort of frolic or orgy with demons, and no step forward into a divine life. As it is with you, so is it with all that I have seen. I will not speak of the immoralities to which Spiritualism has given origin or opportunity. Free love is not a plant indigenous to Spiritualism. It starts in human nature, and grows wherever there is license. The doctrine of "affinities" is as old as the race, and has found its advocates among the beastly of all races and the bad of all religions. I say I will not speak of the immoralities which have been associated with Spiritualism, because they are not peculiar to it; but I say that I cannot perceive that you make the slightest progress intellectually—you or your friends. You have always been busy with these little material phenomena, which have no more spiritual significance or vitality in them than there is in the grunts that come from a pig-sty—not half as much as there is in a concert by Christy's minstrels. Has Spiritualism nothing more in it for you than this? Is this the highest food it has to offer you? Why, you ought to be intellectually a giant by this time. With immortality demonstrated to you, in daily communion with the spiritual world, with vision clarified of all errors and superstitions, you ought to have made advances which would prove to an incredulous world that Spiritualism has in it the seeds at least, of the intellectual millennium. It is not necessary for me to tell you that you have done no such thing. You have been mixed up with two or three fanciful schemes for social improvement, that have not had enough of vitality in them to preserve them from quick degeneration, and these schemes have absorbed all your spiritual activities. Indeed, I think these "circles" have been rather dissipating than edifying to you.

Literature has always been the record and the gauge of every form of civilization, every system of philosophy, and every scheme of religion; and nothing is more certain than that any religion which possesses vitality will permeate and inform all the literature associated with it, and create for itself a literature which is especially the product of its life. Thus, with the Bible for its basis, Christianity has created a literature of its own. An Alexandrian library could not contain the books which cluster around the Bible, deriving from it their sole inspiration and significance, and receiving from it all their power, while there is not a book of any kind written within the pale of Christian civilization which is not modified by it. And literature is but one of the forms of art in which the Christian religion betrays the vitality of its central truths and ideas. There is hardly a department of painting and sculpture and architecture that does not have reference, at some point, to it, while many departments are its direct outgrowth and offspring. It is time that Spiritualism, if it possesses such claims and powers as are ascribed to it, should make its mark on literature and art. Has it done so?

I think that you cannot fail to regard the literature that has been the direct and immediate outgrowth of Spiritualism as, on the whole, of an exceedingly frivolous, weak, and unworthy character. Spiritualism has undertaken to deal with almost all forms of literary art. It has put forth orations, philosophical disquisitions, revelations concerning the unseen world, prophecies of future events, and poetry. These productions purport to come from the spirits of departed men and women, who assume to speak from actual knowledge acquired in the realm of spiritual things. The least that can be assumed by the Spiritualist is that these utterances are the product of minds purified and exalted by freedom from the grosser animal life into which they were originally born, strengthened and invigorated by direct contact with spiritual truth, and inspired by the vision of those realities of which we can only form, through guess and conjecture, the faintest idea. I say that this is the least that can be assumed by the Spiritualist. It is the least that is assumed by you, or any one of your associates, concerning the utterances of your best spiritual correspondents; yet I defy you to point me to a single oration originating in your circles that can compare with those of Webster, or Burke, or Everett; a single philosophical discourse that betrays the brains of a Bacon; a single revelation of the unseen world that can compare with that of John; or a single poem that is not surpassed many times by many poems from the pen of the lamented Mrs. Browning. You are lame in every field in which, in accordance with your theories, you should walk with kingly strides. You cannot hold in contempt the literary judgments of the world; and the literary judgments of the world are against you. It is the decided opinion of those whose opinion you are bound to respect, that your theories of intellectual and spiritual progress beyond the grave are shockingly disproved by the products of the minds which pretend to address us from it. There is nothing in the literature of Spiritualism which, in power and beauty, and practical adaptation to the wants of men, and skilful use of language, can compare with the literature written before Spiritualism made its first rap. Do you doubt it? Look at the alcoves of the scholars and poets of the world, and mark the shelves which your classics occupy. They are not there at all, and their absence is owing to the simple fact that they are not worthy to be there. Literature is catholic. Literary men are not particular as to the source from which great thoughts come, and they will gather where they find them. They have not found them in the literature of Spiritualism. I state this as a fact, which you cannot deny;

and I appeal to the literary men of the world as my witnesses.

In the degree by which Spiritualism has failed to produce a worthy literature of its own, has it failed to incorporate itself as a vital force into any literature. In a few English novels we have seen evidences of its presence, but even there it has furnished only machinery for mysteries and not ideas for life. No poet of power has gone to it for his inspirations. While many literati have been attracted to its marvels, and not a small number of them have acknowledged their faith in the genuineness of its "manifestations," it finds no record in the characteristic products of their pens. And now, in view of all these facts, I declare my full conviction that Spiritualism, notwithstanding all its high pretensions and its ambitious efforts, has imported no new intellectual food into the world, and brought no increment to its intellectual life. Has heaven been opened, my friend, to scatter crumbs and broken victuals to children already fed with bread from the tree of a nobler life? Have the dead come back to prove to you and me that they have only made progress toward, or into, imbecility and idiocy? Have the angels of God forgotten to be wise, and the saints of God learned to be silly? Is a religion, or a system of philosophy, or a revelation of whatever character, good for anything, or worthy of a moment's consideration, which gives us nothing greater and more abounding in vitality than what we have had before—nothing great and vital enough to create a literature of its own, which will command the respect of the world, and find its way through various channels of life into all literature? You have common sense—or used to have. Answer the question.

I remember very well the boast that you and your friends made, a few years ago, that the world was about to witness a new dispensation, through the ministry and the revelations of Spiritualism. We had outgrown Christianity, as the world once outgrew Judaism, you declared, and so, burning up our soiled and worn-out creeds, and casting off the clothing of the Christian church, which had grown too strait for us, we were to emerge into a brighter light and a freer and a nobler life. Well, have your boasts proved to be well grounded? You must not complain that I ask you this question, and say that I do not give you time enough, and refer me to the difficulty of the early steps of Christianity. Spiritualism was born into a very different age from that which witnessed the advent of Christianity. There was no steamboat, no railroad, no telegraph, no universal newspaper, no printing press, to wait upon the early steps of Christianity. The first wail in the little village of Bethlehem that gave notice of the advent of The Redeemer did not reach outside of the walls of the stable where he lay; but through the ministry of modern art—itself the child of Bethlehem's child—the first rap at Rochester was heard throughout the nation. Every appliance of Christian civilization has waited upon the early steps of Spiritualism, and within fifteen years it has been sown wherever steam and lightning can travel, and men can read the language which they speak. It has been free to do what it would. It has published what it would. Prisons and scaffolds have not threatened those who received and entertained and advocated it. It has been patronized by the fashionable and the titled. Royalty itself has lent its eyes and ears to its marvels, and petted the mediums through which they were wrought. It has been brought fairly before the world, and now, what have you to say of the results?

Preliminarily, is it making progress to-day? Does it occupy as large a place in the public mind of this country and of other countries as it did some years ago? Is it winning as many proselytes as it was winning ten years ago? Has it not already called to itself its own, and ceased to be aggressive? Is it not already dying from lack of power to nourish and bless those who have been attracted to it? It is probable that you would not answer these questions as I should, yet it seems to me as if there could be but one answer to them. I know that, as far as my acquaintance reaches, Spiritualism is making neither proselytes nor progress, and that many of those who were once its most earnest defenders have grown cold toward it, or careless of it. It has shown no power to fertilize society, and no disposition to organize society for philanthropic effort. It has originated a few utopian schemes that promised great things for human harmony and happiness, but they have fallen to pieces, light and flimsy as they were, of their own dead weight. I cannot point to anything that Spiritualism is really doing to elevate, purify, and save mankind. I cannot find in it that principle of love which uproots selfishness, or leads the martyr to dare his death of fire.

Now, where is this effete Christianity which was to be displaced by Spiritualism? There never was a period of fifteen years in its history when it made more progress than it has made since Spiritualism was announced. The greatest revival the world ever saw has occurred during that period. It has planted its feet in new fields, and is everywhere aggressive. This Spiritualism, which was to supersede it, has hardly been a fly in the path of its gigantic progress. It is pushing its silent, individual conquests, and organizing its forces in the wilds of the West, on the shores of the Pacific, in Australia, and among the heathen nations of the world. It is gaining new victories near the centres of its power. It gives no sign of decay. It is more and more widely recognized as the grand, saving and reforming power of the world—as a religion to live by and die by. It finds its way into governmental institutions. It more and more pervades every kind of literature, and you know that there is not a good thing in Spiritualism that Christianity had not previously promulgated.

There are some of your friends who will deny that Spiritualism opposes Christianity. Indeed, there are some who claim that they are really the only enlightened Christians in the world, Spiritualism having interpreted Christianity to them. You are too honest to tell me this, I know, because you have talked very differently to me many times. You know that if Spiritualism is not in opposition to Christianity, as a system of religion and of salvation, there is nothing in it whatever. You know, and so do your friends, that Spiritualism is at least in opposition to that form of Christianity which prevails in the world, and which marks its progress by such marvellous evidences of its vitality and power.

My friend, you are eating husks, when you might have corn. Cut the delusion loose, for it is a dying thing. There is nothing more in it for you or the world—no more food, nor inspiration, nor light, nor life, nor blessing. All the good fellows are going my way. Come and join them.

THE EIGHTH LETTER.

To Benjamin Franklin Jones, Mechanic.

CONCERNING HIS HABITUAL ABSENCE FROM CHURCH ON SUNDAY.

I HAVE often wondered why you and so many who are engaged in mechanical pursuits should be so skeptical in all matters lying outside of the domain of material things. There seems to be something in the constitution of the mechanical mind, or something in the nature of mechanical pursuits, which tends to infidelity. It is notorious that, as a class, the mechanics of this country, and particularly those who are engaged in such branches as call for the most ingenuity and skill, are given to unbelief. I cannot explain this. I see the fact, as it exists in manufacturing communities and in the larger cities, and am entirely at a loss to account for it. Why is it that constant dealing with the laws of matter and second causes should so induce materialism, and so hide the Great First Cause, I do not know. I only know that the coldest infidels I have ever known—men the most utterly faithless in spiritual things—men skeptical on all subjects which touch religion and immortality, and revelation and God—are mechanics, and that there seems to be something in their pursuits, or in their mental constitution, which makes them so.

The number of these men in every New England community is large. We are a manufacturing people, and the best and most influential minds in nearly all our manufacturing towns are those of mechanics. I have been surprised at the contempt in which religion and its institutions are held in some New England towns, where it is supposed that both are honored in an unusual degree. The truth is that, throughout New England, not more than one third of the people go to church, or have anything to do with its support; and that third is very largely composed of farmers and merchants. The mechanical and manufacturing interests, notwithstanding their great magnitude, contribute comparatively little to the maintenance of the institutions of Christianity. None are more aware of the truth of the statements which I make than Christian mechanics, because they are constantly thrown into the society of those of their own class whose cold and sneering infidelity, and whose habitual disregard of the

Sabbath and all Christian institutions, are themes of constant sorrow or annoyance to them. I am sorry to believe that you add one to the number of these faithless men, and particularly sorry, because you have such natural strength of mind that you cannot fail to have great influence upon those who are nearest you—upon your companions and your family. But I must leave these general remarks, for I began with the intention to say something to you upon your habit of staying away from church on Sundays.

You told a friend of mine the other day that you had not put your foot inside of a church for ten years. You made the statement, he informed me, in a tone which indicated contempt not only for the church itself and the religion which it represents, but for all the men and women who attend it. Now I like your frankness. There is something in your position which I cannot but respect. It is different from that of the majority of those who spend their Sundays in laziness or pleasure. When they are questioned with relation to their very questionable courses, they take the position of culprits at once, and make their excuses, always, however, protesting that they have the most profound respect for religion and its institutions. They make a merit of this respect, and put it forward as a substitute for the thing itself. Fools may be taken in by this sort of talk, but God and wise men can only have contempt for those who pretend to honor a religion whose institutions they treat with persistent neglect.

If we speak to some of these men about their neglect of attendance upon the Sunday ministrations of the church, they will say that they can worship God as well in the fields as they can in the sanctuary,—that they can commune with Him quite as well alone, among the beaŭties of nature, as in the great congregation, surrounded by ribbons and artificial flowers. As independent propositions, these may be sound. I will not controvert them; but when these men put them forward, they do it for the purpose of skulking behind them, and they know very well that they have no relation to their case. They know that they never worship God in the fields, and that they would be frightened at the thought of any actual communion with Him. Others will denounce the impurities and imperfections of the church, or find fault with the minister, or certain of the leading members. All kinds of apologies are put forward by these poor men to delude themselves and their neighbors with the belief that they are really better than those who go to church—that they have, at least, quite as much respect for religion as those who do.

All this talk disgusts me, for I know that there is no sincerity in it. When a man tells me that he respects religion, I want to see him prove it in some practical way. If he really respects religion, he will give his life to it, and, as the smallest possible proof of respect that he can render, he will scrupulously attend upon its ordinances, and show to the world the side upon which he wishes his influence to count. No, when men tell me that they respect religion and offer in evidence only their studied and persistent absence from all Christian ministrations, I have simply to respond that I do not respect them. They are a set of hypocrites and humbugs. They talk about the hypocrisy of the church! There is not such another set of hypocrites in America, as those who, while professing to respect Christianity, devote the Christian Sabbath to their own selfish ease or convenience, and regularly shun the assemblages of Christian men and women. Sometimes they try to prove their sincerity by throwing in their wives and children. They will tell people that they hire a pew, and dress their wives and children for the public, that they are willing that they should attend church, and that they have too much respect for religion to stand in anybody's way, while by every Sunday's example, they plainly declare to their wives and children that they regard the church and the religion which it represents as unworthy of the attention of a rational man.

I repeat, then, that there is something in your position which I respect. You have brought yourself to the belief that Christianity is a delusion—a cheat. You have no respect for religion, and do not hesitate to express your contempt for it. All preaching is blarney and cant to you; all prayer is blatant nonsense addressed to a phantom of the imagination. Practically, your companions in absence from the church on Sunday occupy your most decidedly irreligious position, and their weakly lingering belief in the truth of Christianity, or in the possibility of its truth, (which is all their "respect" means,) might as well, for any practical purpose, be disbelief. You are really better than those who pretend to respect religion, and who treat it with the same contempt that you do, because you are not a hypocrite. I address you then as the most respectable and decent man of your class.

My desire is to give you one or two good reasons for going to church which do not depend upon the authenticity of Christianity, or upon the sacredness of the Christian Sabbath at all. My first reason is that unless a man puts himself into a fine shirt, polished boots, and good clothes once a week, and goes out into the public, he is almost certain to sink into semi-barbarism. You know that unless you do this on Sunday, you cannot do it at all, for you labor all the week. There is nothing like isolation to work degeneration in a man. There is nothing like standing alone, with no place in the machinery of society, to tone down one's self-respect. You must be aware that you are not in sympathy with society. You are looked upon as an outsider, because you refuse to come into contact with society on its broadest and best ground. I tell you it is a good thing for a man to wash his face clean, and put on his best clothes, and walk to the house of God with his wife and children on Sundays, whether he believes in Christianity or not. The church is a place where, at the least, good morals are inculcated, and where the vices of the community are denounced. You can afford to stand by so much of the church, and, by doing so, say "Here am I and here are mine, with a stake in the welfare of society, and an interest in the good morals of society." My friend, this little operation gone through with every Sunday would give you self-respect, help you to keep your head above water, and bring you into sympathy with the best society the world possesses. A man needs to beautify himself with good clothes occasionally to assure himself that he is not brother to the beast by the side of which he labors during six days of every seven, and he needs particularly to feel that he has place and consideration in clean society.

Another reason why you should go to church on Sunday is that you need the intellectual nourishment and stimulus which you can only get there. I suppose that you do not often consider the fact that the greatest amount of genuine thinking done in the world is done by preachers. I suppose you may never have reflected that, in the midst of all this din of business, and clashing of various interests—in the midst of the clamors and horrors of war, the universal pursuit of amusements, and the vanities and inanities of fashion, and the indulgence of multitudinous vices, there is a class of self-denying men, of the best education and the best talents and habits, who, in their quiet rooms, are thinking and writing upon the purest and noblest themes which can engage any mind. Among these men may be found the finest minds which the age knows—the most splendid specimens of intellectual power that the world contains. The bright consummate flower of our American college system is the American ministry. Among these men are many who are slow—stupid, if you insist upon it—but there is not one in one thousand of them who does not know more than you do. You can learn something of them all, while some of them possess more brains and more available intellectual power than you and all your relatives combined. I tell you that if you suppose the American pulpit to be contemptible, you are very much mistaken. You have staid away from it for ten years. During all these ten years I have attended its weekly ministrations, and I have a better right to speak about it than you have, because I know more about it. I tell you that I have received during these ten years more intellectual nourishment and stimulus from the pulpit than from all other sources combined, yet my every-day pursuits are literary while yours are not.

There is something in the pursuits of working men —I mean of men who follow handicraft—which renders some intellectual feeding on Sunday peculiarly necessary. You work all day, and when you get home at night, you can do nothing but read the news, and indulge in neighborhood gossip. You are obliged to rise early in the morning, and that makes it necessary that you should go to bed early at night. You really have no time for intellectual culture except on Sunday, and then you are too dull and tired to sit down to a book. You always go to sleep over any book that taxes your brain at all. You know that there is nothing but the living voice which can hold your attention, and you know that that voice can only be heard in the pulpit. The working man who shuns the pulpit on the Sabbath, voluntarily relinquishes the only regularly available intellectual nourishment of his life. You need not tell me that the pulpit has no intellectual nourishment for you. I know better. Philosophy, casuistry, history, metaphysics, science, poetry—these all are at home in the pulpit. All high moralities are taught there. All sweet charities are inculcated there.

There are more argument and illustration brought to the support and enforcement of religious truths than all the other intellectual magazines of the world have at command; and, quarrel with the facts as you may, you must go to church on Sunday, and hear the preaching, or be an intellectual starveling. Your brain is just as certain to degenerate—your intellect is just as certain to grow dull—under this habit of staying at home from church, as a plant is to grow pale when hidden away from the sun.

But you respond that you will not attend church because you do not believe in the doctrines that are preached there. Do you refuse to attend a political meeting which a gifted speaker is to address, because you are not of his way of thinking? Do you stay away from the lecture of a man who has brains, because you cannot indorse his sentiments? Why, you are behind the age, man. The most popular lecturers of America have for years been those who have represented the principles and sentiments of a small minority. Intellectual men have maintained their place upon the platform when their persons and their principles were held in abhorrence by the masses whom they addressed. It is not necessary for me to mention names, to prove this statement, for the facts are too fresh and too notorious. Do you decline to attend a circus because the performers differ with you as to the number of horses it is proper for a man to ride at one time? Is it possible that you, who have been charging bigotry upon the church and its representatives so long, are a bigoted man? Is it possible that you, who have denounced the American Christian ministry for intolerance, are intolerant yourself? It looks like it.

My friend, you are lame in this matter. Your position is a very weak one. It is not based in any principle—it is based in prejudice. Besides, you are not truthful when you say that the utterances of the pulpit generally are incredible. I have been a constant attendant at church all my life, and I declare without hesitation that three quarters of the sermons I have heard have been other than doctrinal sermons. The majority of the sermons preached have their foundation in the eternal principles of right—in the broad moralities to which you and every other decent man subscribes. You know that, as a system of morals, Christianity is faultless. You know that if the world should live up to the morals of Christianity—we will say nothing about it as a system of religion—there would be no murder, no war, no slavery, no drunkenness, no licentiousness, no lying, no stealing, no cheating, no wrong,—that everywhere men would walk in peace and concord and fraternal affection, and that the golden rule would be the universal rule of life. The pulpit is the spot of all others in the world where, through the wonderful agency of the human voice, these morals are taught; and do you tell me that you will not go to church because you do not believe in what is taught there? You do believe in at least three quarters of the teachings of the pulpit. You do yourself great wrong by holding yourself aloof from an institution which would not only nourish your intellect, but instruct and confirm you in those moralities which are the only safeguard of that society which numbers among its members your wife and children.

Perhaps you can afford, or feel that you can afford, to teach your children that Christianity, as a system of religion, is a cheat, but you cannot afford to confound with it, and condemn with it, the moralities of Christianity. You cannot afford to teach your children by words or deeds that the great mass of the teachings of the pulpit are unworthy of consideration; for their safety, their respectability, their prosperity, their happiness, all depend upon the adoption and practice of Christian morals. Do *you* teach them Christian morals? Are *you* careful to sit down on the Sabbath, or at any other time, and instruct them in those moralities that are essential to the right and happy issue of their lives? My friend, you have not the face to do any such thing, for your position will not permit you to do it without shame. Well, if you refuse to do it, who will? Unhappily your wife is quite as much under your influence as your children, and unless those children go to church on Sunday, they will get no instruction in Christian morals whatever, except such as they may pick up at the public schools.

These children of yours are not to blame for being in the world. They came forth from nothingness in answer to your call, and they are on your hands. You are responsible to them, at least, for their right training. You are in personal honor bound to give them such instruction in morals as will tend to preserve to them health of body and mind, and honorable relations with society. How will you do it? By telling them that church-going is foolishness, and Sabbath-keeping nonsense, and the teachings of the pulpit only the tricks of priestcraft and the amusement of blockheads? No, sir. You must take these children by the hand and lead them to church, and show that there are, at least, some things that come from the pulpit which you respect. It will not be enough that you send them and their mother. You must go with them, for, if you do not, they will soon learn the realities of the pulpit, and, in learning them, learn to pity you, and to hold your intolerance in contempt. You must stand by the pulpit as the great teacher of private and public morality, or do an awful injustice to the children for whose life and healthy education you are responsible.

THE NINTH LETTER.

To Washington Allston Jones.

CONCERNING THE POLICY OF MAKING HIS BRAINS MARKETABLE.

JUDGING from recent conversations with you, and from many things I have heard about you, you are not satisfied with the results of your life, thus far. You have tried various fields of effort, and have failed of the success you sought in all. You know my honest friendship for you, and the measurable respect which I entertain not only for your intellectual gifts, but for that high ideal of art and its mission which has been the only bar to your reward. You wrote a novel, which failed, simply because you refused to write one which would succeed. You erected a standard in your own soul, bowed to your standard, and then was disgusted because the humanity upon which you had turned your back would not applaud your doings. You wrote a poem, classical without a doubt—powerful and beautiful in its way beyond question—but, somehow, the poem had no point of sympathy with the age which you believed ought to receive and love it. Behind these two books you sat in imperial pride, disgusted with a world which seemed so little in knowledge and so low in feeling—so unable to appreciate you, and so ready to give its applause to men of slenderer faculty and shallower motive. Will you permit me to say to you now, before it is too late, that the world will never come to you, and that you must go to the world or die voiceless?

My friend, the world is not in want, just at this time, of life-size portraits in oil, with all their stately conventional accompaniments. The world happens to want photographs, and will have nothing but photographs. You choose to stand by your pigments and your canvas and your camel's hair, and to starve, while all the world rushes by you to patronize the sun. You imagine that it would degrade you to have anything to do with photographs. You would not make one—you would not color one—you would not touch one with one of your fingers, because your idea of art, or what you choose to consider art, is so high, that you could have nothing to do with the production of a photograph without a sense of humiliation. You will die rather than disgrace the art to which you are in honor married, and degrade the standard you have erected for yourself. Die, my friend, if it will be any satisfaction to you; but the world will never thank you for it, and, moreover, will vote you a fool for your voluntary sacrifice. The only way for you is to meet the want of the world and make photographs—make the best photographs the world has seen—so that it shall come to you and ask you to do it favors, and beg the privilege of paying you much honor and much money.

I confess to you again that I have a measurable respect for that ideal of art which refuses all compromise with popular prejudice, and, standing alone, strives to compel the homage of the world, and failing, stands in self-complacent pride to pity and despise those who will not bow to it. Yet this ideal, upon which the issue of your life seems to be turning, has in it, to a fatal degree, the element of selfishness. My friend, what is art but a minister? What is art but a vehicle by which you may transport the life which is in you to the souls by which you are surrounded—for their good, and not for yours? Cut off from its relations to life—to the life which produces it, and that to which it is addressed—standing by itself—what is art but a phantom?—a nothing with a name? God has endowed you with intellectual wealth. He has given you great powers, and set you upon a throne where you can reason and judge and reach outward and upward into great imaginations; he has given you the power to speak and to sing. For what purpose? Is it that you may selfishly shut this wealth of yours into a coffer, and close the lips of your utterance, from obedience to a standard of art which has more reference to you than to the world to which you owe service? You are rich and must dispense. Who gave you your wealth? Is it for you to stand and higgle with the world about the form or style in which it shall receive your gifts? Is it for you to declare that the world shall have none of your expression, unless it be accepted in a certain form, which form shall have supreme consideration?

You have carried your reverence for your idea of art and your contempt for those who will not regard it so far that you cannot speak with patience of those who succeed in the fields which have witnessed your failure. You have learned to despise those whom the world applauds, because you think the world's applause can only be won by treachery to art. This contempt for those who succeed is the logical result of your own failure; and now you sit alone, in selfish pride, a martyr, as you suppose, to your better ideal and your higher aim, the world unconscious meanwhile that you have in you the power to move and bless it. You have told me that you distrust a book which sells, and have spoken with undisguised contempt of men who carry "marketable brains," as you were pleased to call them.

And now we get at our subject. What are brains good for that are not marketable? My belief is that a man who has brains is in duty bound to make them marketable. My position is that unless mind, under Christian direction and control, is marketable, it is useless; and you must permit me to use the word marketable in the largest sense. The world is as we find it —not as we would have it. We write, we speak, we paint, we give utterance to all forms of art, in order to make the world richer and better; and unless the world will receive what we utter, and take it into its life, it is not benefited, and our utterance is a failure. There are doubtless a few great souls, laboring in some difficult departments of art, that must labor for the few, and through these few find their way to the world, but these are exceptional cases. Yours is not one, for you have undertaken only to address the world at large, and it is your fault that you have failed. You would not take the world as you found it. You intended that the world should take you as it found you. You did not go to the world to sell, throwing yourself into its markets, but you stood at your own door, determined to compel the world to come to you and buy. The world did not come, and I do not blame it.

In intellectual no less than in commercial affairs, the market is the first consideration. The manufacturer never adopts one style of fabric as that to which alone his efforts at production shall be devoted, but studies the market, and shifts his machinery and modifies his material in accordance with the indications of the market. We hear of certain preachers who preach great sermons, such as a few only love to hear, or have the power to remember and appropriate. They have no right to preach such sermons. If they have any gold in them, they should reduce it to coin that will pass current with the people. There is a stiff and stilted set in occupation of many of the American pulpits, who suspect a preacher who is very popular, and hold in contempt him who places himself in thorough sympathy with the crowd around him that he may reach and hold them, and who are particularly disgusted with what they call "sensation preaching." It seems better to them to preach to small congregations than to draw large houses by making their preaching marketable. Is this being all things to all men, that they may save some? Not at all. It is being one thing to a few men, whether they save any or not. St. Paul understood the matter of making his intellectual gifts and his preaching marketable. We know writers of magnificent powers—some of them who are certainly very greatly your superiors in mental acquisitions—who are burying their gifts in books that find no buyers. These men might as well be horseblocks, so far as the world is concerned. They are doing nothing for the world. They have not consulted its market, and appear to know and care nothing about its wants. We know orators who never let themselves down to minister to the desire of those whom they address to be melted and moved, but who, with stately dignity, insist on being rational and dull, and on driving from them those whom they desire to hold.

You, my friend, sympathize with all these men, but do you not see how much a selfish pride lies at the basis of their action? I give you and them credit for that self-respect which shrinks from the tricks of the mountebank and the demagogue, but I charge you and them with a pride which is not consistent with the position of the artist as a minister of life. With all your nobleness of nature, you have never been able to conceive of a higher motive of action, in a literary man, than the ambition to achieve literary distinction. You do not understand how a man can undertake a literary enterprise which has not literary reputation for its object; and when some book is uttered for the simple purpose of doing good, by one who has it in him to do great things for himself—a book which does not even pretend to literary merit beyond that which lies in adapting means to ends—you curl your lip in contempt for his voluntary degradation. He writes for a market, and the world accepts him, and he does the world good; and if he did not write for a market, the world would spurn him as it spurns you; and he would be deprived as you are of the privilege of doing the world good.

I suppose you hug to yourself the delusion that you are in advance of your age, and that what it fails to appreciate, posterity will receive at its full value. To leave out of consideration the selfishness of this fancy—as if you and your reputation were the only things to be taken into account—let me assure you that the coming age will have its own heroes to look after, and will stand a very small chance of stumbling upon your dead novel and your still-born poem. Sir, the only way for you to win the reputation which I know you desire, is to throw your life—your thinking and acting self—into this age, as a power to uplift and mould and bless it. You must come into the market. You must shape your utterances to the want of the times. You must be content to work for others, forgetful of yourself, and to give to men, in cups from which they will drink it, that life with which God has filled you.

But you despise your age. The age has not treated

you well. The age is vulgar and low and rude and ungrateful. The age is mercenary and immoral. Your wounded self-love has misled you, sir. You are living in the greatest age of the world, and your soul only needs to be attuned to its great movements and events to find itself coined into words for their majestic music.

"Every age
Appears to souls who live in it (ask Carlyle)
Most unheroic. Ours, for instance, ours!
The thinkers scout it and the poets abound
Who scorn to touch it with a finger-tip:
A pewter age—mixed metal, silver-washed;
An age of scum, spooned off the richer past;
An age of patches for old gaberdines;
An age of mere transition, meaning nought
Except that what succeeds must shame it quite,
If God please."

And now, as I have broached Mrs. Browning upon this point, I will go farther and let her sing the rest of my paragraph:

"Nay, if there's room for poets in the world
A little overgrown (I think there is),
Their sole work is to represent the age—
Their age, not Charlemagne's—this live, throbbing age,
That brawls, cheats, maddens, calculates, aspires,
And spends more passion, more heroic heat,
Betwixt the mirrors of its drawing rooms,
Than Roland with his knights at Roncesvalles.
To flinch from modern varnish, coat, or flounce,
Cry out for togas and the picturesque,
Is fatal—foolish too. * * *

"Never flinch,
But, still unscrupulously epic, catch
Upon the burning lava of a song
The full-veined, heaving, double-breasted age;
That, when the next shall come, the men of that
May touch the impress with reverent hand, and say,
'Behold—behold the paps we all have sucked!'"

"This is living art,
Which thus presents and thus records true life."

Do what you can to make your age great. Be alike its minister and its mouthpiece. Give yourself to your age, and your age will take care of you, and the ages to come will be the guardians of your fame.

When you spoke to me of "marketable brains," I understood you of course to use the phrase in a lower sense than that in which I have used it. I have not adopted your meaning, simply because it walks in the shadow of mine. A man who adapts the products of his brain to the real wants of the world, is the man who sells his books and makes money by them. You ought to be sensible enough to know that a man who writes from no higher motive than the desire to win money, cannot meet the wants of the world, and that he who writes a marketable book must necessarily be something better than a mercenary wretch who would sell all that is godlike in him for gold. Yet I will admit that the desire to win bread—nay, the ambition to acquire a competent wealth—is, in its subordinate place, a worthy motive in impelling the artist to make his brains marketable. Commerce puts its brains into the market, and nobody cries out "shame," or hints at humiliation. The brains of all this working, trading, scheming world are in the market. These "marketable brains" are the pabulum of progress everywhere; and a writer is good for nothing for the world who does not understand what it is to work for a living—what it is to expend life for the means of continuing life. Nay, I would go farther, and say that God has, by direct intent, compelled the worker in all departments of art to make his brains marketable, under penalty of starving.

I know, my friend, that this is all very disgusting to you. You feel that the artist ought to be king, and that grateful men should only be too glad to do homage and bring gifts to him. You are wrong. The people are kings, and you are their servant. The law announced by the Great Teacher on this point is universal, and without exception. A man is felt to be great only by reason of his power to minister to the life around him. Life licks the hand that feeds it. You think it a degradation to go to the world with your brains, adapting their product to the popular want, and taking your pay in the currency of the country; but it is this or something worse. Think of those kings of the old English literature, who were obliged to sit and sneak in the anterooms of nobles, and beg the patronage of the rich and great, and become lickspittles for the sake of the influence that would sell their books, and give them position, and furnish them with bread to starve on and a garret to die in. The world will not buy what it does not want, and you are unreasonable if you blame it. You thirst for the world's praise, you need its money, you really envy the success of others, and because praise and money and success are denied you, you button your coat to your chin, turn up your nose to the world, and, " grand, gloomy, and peculiar," stand apart.

You mistake entirely if you suppose the world to be a contemptible master; and this failure to appreciate the world—this persistent under-estimate of the world—which you and all of your class entertain, is enough to account for your failure. The world deals with practical life, and is guided by experience and common sense. The world is at work to win bread and raiment and shelter. The world digs the field, and searches the seas, and trades, and manufactures, and builds railroads and telegraphs and ships, and prints and reads newspapers. The world is full of the cares of government. The world fights battles and pays taxes. The world is under a great pressure of care and work. This working, trading, fighting, careful world holds within itself the great, vital forces of society, the practical interests of humanity, the wisest, brightest, noblest minds that live. And this world, for which you have such contempt, is the only competent judge of the artist, and is always the final judge of art. "The light of the public square will test its value," said Michael Angelo to the young sculptor whose work he was examining. The remark was the bow of a respectful servant to his master. You can write for dillettanti if you choose—for an audience "fit, though few"—for the fellows of the mutual admiration society—and they will praise you; but you know that if you fail to get hold of this world which you affect to despise, you are powerless and without reward as a literary man.

As I think of your kingly gifts of intellect, and of the power there is in you to bless mankind, art itself appears before me in the likeness of Him who wore the seamless robe among humble disciples, and the crown of thorns between thieves. Ah! when art becomes the mediator between genius and the world, then does it answer to its noblest ideal, and confer the greatest glory upon the artist. You, in your realm, are almost as incomprehensible and unapproachable by the world as God was, before He expressed His love and His practical good will through the gift of The Beloved. He had wrought augustly in the heavens, and filled the earth with glory. He had crowded immensity with the tokens of His power and the expressions of His majestic thought; but the world did not see Him—would not receive Him—regarded Him without reverence. Why should He not despise the world? Why, falling back upon the dignity of His Godhood, and sufficient for himself, did He not spurn the race which so disgraced itself and Him? Ah! He pitied. He respected the characteristics of the nature He had made. He sent the choicest child of His Infinite Bosom down into the world to wear its humblest garb, and eat its homeliest fare, and perform its meanest offices, and die its most terrible and disgraceful death, that the world might drink through Him the life of the Everlasting Father. My friend, send your mediator into the world. Send the child of your bosom, clad in humble garments—charged only with a mission of love and practical good will to men. Let me assure you that you can only bring the world to love you and learn of you by making it the partaker of your life through some expression of art which it can appropriate. No matter if it die. It shall rise again, and when it rises, rise to you, drawing all men unto it and unto you.

THE TENTH LETTER.

To Rev. Jeremiah Jones, D.D.

CONCERNING THE FAILURE OF HIS PULPIT MINISTRY.

I NEVER should have undertaken this letter to you, had I not been requested to do so by one of your professional brethren. It is not a pleasant thing to find fault with people, particularly with those whose faults are the results of natural organization. My object in finding fault at any time, with any person, is reform; and you can never reform. You cannot make yourself over again, into something different and better; and this ink of mine will be wasted, unless it shall address other eyes than yours. The assurance that other eyes will be interested in what I have to say to you determines me to write this letter.

Surveying the American pulpit, I find it occupied by men who can legitimately be divided into two great classes, and these, for the present purpose, I will call the poetical and the unpoetical. I am not sure that these designations are sufficiently definite, or even sufficiently suggestive, but I can tell you what I mean by them. The class which I denominate poetical is composed of men who possess imagination, strong and tender sympathies, profound insight into human character and motive, and the power to attract to themselves the affections of those around them. These men possess also what we term individuality in an unusual degree—a quality which carries with it the power to transmute truth into life—to resolve systems into character—to appropriate, digest, and assimilate all spiritual food whatsoever, so that when they preach they do not preach as the mouthpieces of a school, or a sect, or a system, but as revelators and promulgators of a life. These are the preachers who touch men, because they preach out of their own life and experience. These are the men who speak from the heart and reach the heart—the men who possess what, for lack of a better name, we call magnetism. The unpoetical class may roughly be defined by the statement that they are the opposites of the poetical. They have no imagination; they are not men of strong and tender sympathies; they do not possess fine insight (though some of them possess a degree of cunning which is mistaken for it); they have not the power to attract to themselves the affections of those around them; they do not possess true individuality (though they may have peculiarities or idiosyncracies which pass for it); and, in their utterances, they are little more than the mouthpieces of the systems and schools to which they are attached.

To the latter class I assign you without the slightest hesitation, because nature has placed you in it. I have no expectation that you will ever be different from what you are. It is possible that some terrible affliction or some great humiliation will soften your character, and develop your heart, and quicken your sympathies, but I could hardly pray for such discipline as would be necessary to revolutionize your constitution. No sir; you will probably live and die the same sort of a man you always have been—useful in some respects, self-complacent in all respects—an irreproachable, unlóvable, sound, solid, dogmatic doctor of divinity.

I give you credit for an honest Christian character and purpose, but I should be false to my convictions should I fail to tell you that I consider you and all who are like you to be out of place in the Christian pulpit. Your religion is mostly a matter of intellect. You are fond of preaching doctrine. You delight in what you are pleased to denominate theology. You rejoice in a controversy. You speak as by authority. You denounce sin, as if you had never sinned, and never expected to sin. You unfold what you call "the scheme of salvation" as if it were a grand contrivance of the Supreme Being to circumvent Himself—a marvellous invention by which He is enabled to harmonize His justice with His pity. You have a "system of truth" to promulgate, and, in your mind, it seems essential that this system should be accepted in all its parts as the condition of salvation. You are, indeed, the special guardian of the orthodoxy of your region. Alas! for the poor candidate for the Christian ministry who may be obliged to pass under your examination! Alas! for any person who may presume to decide that a man can be a Christian without embracing your "system of truth," or that religion is not quite as much a matter of the brains as of the heart! You lug along into this present age, to its scandal and its shame, to the detriment and disgrace of the Christian cause, the old Puritan idea that assent to a creed—that belief in certain dogmas—has more to do with the soundness of a man's Christianity than anything else. You do not ask, first and foremost, in your inquiries concerning a man, whether his life is pure—pious toward God and loving and benevolent toward men—but whether he is sound in his "views." At this very moment, while you are reading these words, you are wondering, not whether I am a Christian man, loving and serving God and men, but whether I am orthodox or heterodox in my "views;" and because I hold your frigid scholasticism in contempt, you regard me as "loose" in my "views," and, on the whole, dangerous in my teachings. Tell me, doctor, if it is not so? Have you not been troubled more with doubts about my orthodoxy, while reading this paragraph, than anything else?

Will you be offended if I reveal to you the nature of your Sabbath ministrations, and endeavor to show you why you cannot hope to accomplish very much for your Master? Your manner is not humble—your spirit is not humble. You do not enter your church on Sunday morning crushed with a sense of your responsibility—feeling the need of aid and inspiration —filled with tender reverence toward God and love toward man. Your utterances are those of a self-sufficient man. Your prayers touch nobody. They are full of sonorous phrases culled from the sacred text; they abound in passages of information addressed to the Deity; they embrace all the objects of Christian solicitude and labor; they range the earth through all the degrees of latitude and longitude for subjects; the sailor, the soldier, the heathen, the Jews, the Roman Catholics and all other errorists, the foreign missionaries, the home missionaries, the civil authorities—all these come in by catalogue. These broad generalities of petition, which do not grow, as you very well know, out of any immediate impulse of desire, but only out of a general impression of desirableness, have not the slightest power to lead a congregation in genuine prayer. The thing sounds well. The words are well chosen and well pronounced, but they do not lift a heart to its Maker, or give voice to the aspirations of a single soul.

Your sermon is like your prayer, and carries with it the idea that you are safe, and comparatively independent. It is as if you were to stand in your pulpit, and say: "Here am I, Rev. Jeremiah Jones, D. D., safe, by the grace of God, forever, with a message to deliver. Repent and believe what I believe, and you will be saved; refuse to repent and believe what I believe, and you will be damned. Take things in my way, see things as I see them, adopt my opinions and my system, and you will be all right. If you do not, then you will be all wrong, and I wash my hands of all responsibility for your destruction." Salvation would seem, in your scheme, to be a matter of machinery. You preach just what you were taught to preach at the theological seminary, and have not taken a single step in advance. It is the same old brain-stuff, unsoftened by a better love, unfertilized by a better experience, without life or the power to enrich life. You put before your hearers a skeleton, and hold them responsible for not seeing and admitting that it is a beautiful form of life. You give them a system and a scheme, when they need a life and a heart. You insist on driving them by threats to Him who, with a different spirit and different policy, said "Come unto me."

Do not understand me to blame you for all this, for you cannot very well help it. I only state the matter in detail, to prove that the pulpit is not the place for you. You are honest enough, but you have no sensibility. You have mind enough, but you have none of that poetic or spiritual insight which enables other men to seize the essence of that scheme of truths with whose adjustment into form and system you so constantly busy yourself. I once entered the study of a preacher who had been for three months out of public employment, and who, to demonstrate to me his industry, assured me that he had written during that period thirty-six sermons. Indeed, he showed me the pile. Now there was a job which you could have done just as well as he, but neither you nor he, nor any other man who could do it, is fit to write a sermon at all. Moved by no special want of the souls around him, taking no suggestions from the living time, he wrote sermons—very sound sermons, doubtless—but sermons with no more power in them to move men than there is in a mathematical proposition. You seem to feel that the truth is the truth, and that if you promulgate it with an honest purpose, it is all that is necessary. Men occasionally find their way into your pulpit, however, to whom your congregation give their hearts before they have uttered ten sentences, and why? The heart instinctively acknowledges the credentials of its teacher. There is something about some men, in the pulpit, which draws my heart to them at once. I know by their bearing, by the sound of their voices, by every emanation of their personality, that their hearts are on a sympathetic level with all humanity—that they are bowing tearfully under their own burden while they help to bear mine—that they are my fellows in temptation, in struggle, in aspiration.

This poetic instinct—this power to reach through words and phrases, and forms and types and figures, and to grasp the naked truths of which they are only the representatives—is essential to any man who feeds the people. You are fond of creeds and catechisms; and those who listen to you are instructed in creeds and catechisms; but you might just as hopefully undertake to make a living tree out of dry chips, as a living Christian out of creeds and catechisms. This poetic instinct or power is the solvent of creeds and catechisms—the gastric juice that softens them into chyle, and the absorbents that suck from them their vital fluid for the soul's nourishment. But why do I talk to you about this poetic faculty? You do not understand me. You do not comprehend me at all. You think that I am foggy and fanciful—transcendental and nonsensical; but it is you—stolid pretender to solidity and sound sense—who are foggy and fanciful. You think and call yourself a matter-of-fact man, when you are only a matter-of-form man. The poet is the man who touches facts. The poet is the man of common sense, who finds and reveals the inner life and meaning of things? The true poet in a free pulpit is a man in his place, and no other man is fit for the place. When the true poet speaks from the pulpit, the people hear; and they will hear gladly no other man. He is the only man who can reveal a congregation to itself. The great charm of The Great Teacher to the woman at the well was His power to tell her all the things that ever she did, and that was her sole recommendation of Him to those of her friends whom she invited into His presence.

There are not so many preachers of your class in the world now as there were once, thank God! It was this brain Christianity—this intellectualism—this scholasticism—that gave root to those great controversies and schisms which disgraced Christianity, alike in the judgment of history and the eyes of a faithless world. Pride of theological opinion, sectarian partisanship, strifes of words, splittings of hairs, formalisms,—these have been the curse of Christianity and the clog upon its progress in all ages. You and those who are like you have made a complicated and difficult thing of that which is exquisitely simple. You have surrounded that fountain which flows with a volume of sparkling bounty for the cleansing and the healing of all humanity, with hedges of words and forms, and conditions and prejudices; yet you are too blind to see it. But I see your class fading out, and another and a better coming in, and I mark with gratitude the change in the general aspect of the Christian enterprise. The differences between sects are growing small by degrees and beautifully less. Brother grasps the hand of brother across the chasms which the fathers made. Names do not separate as they once did those whom the common reception of the vital truths of Christianity has made one. Love unites those whom logic and learning have long divided. And you, sir, with your dry doctrinal discourses, your array of redemptive machinery, your denunciations and threatenings, your fulminations against opposing sects, your pride of opinion and your hard and unpoetic nature, are out of place in a pulpit that is already far in advance of you.

I recently addressed a letter to an intelligent relative of yours concerning his habit of staying away from the church on the Sabbath. I found serious fault with him for his delinquencies in this respect. I undertook to present to him sufficient reasons for reform, and prominently among those reasons I stated that he needed the intellectual stimulus which, in his circumstances, he would only secure by attendance on the ministrations of the pulpit. I do not retract what I said to him at all. I should advise him to hear you preach, rather than to hear nobody, spending his Sabbaths in idleness; yet I cannot hide from you the fact that you and those who are like you are responsible to a great extent for the thinly attended Christian meetings of the Sabbath. I cannot help feeling that those preachers who find themselves without power to draw men to them by the beauty of their lives and characters, and by the adaptedness of their teachings to the popular want, and by that magnetism of poetic or spiritual sympathy which is the heavenly baptism, are doing more than they imagine to depopulate the churches. I confess to no small degree of sympathy with those who prefer staying at home to hearing you preach; for though I am sometimes stirred intellectually by you, I am never moved religiously and spiritually.

Look at the churches with me for a moment, my reverend friend, and mark what you see. Here is a church with a man in the pulpit of great intellectual gifts and excellent scholarship. His sermons are models of English composition. He is known in all the churches as a sound man. Look over his congregation: two, three, four, in a pew—old men, steady men, pious women—some asleep—all decorous. You will see the same sight fifty-two Sundays of the year. The teaching is good enough, but there is no motion. The instruction is sound, but there is no impulse. How many respectable, sleepy, sound preachers and churches do you suppose there are in this country which show no change from Sabbath to Sabbath and from year to year, and which make no aggressive inroads upon the worldly life which environs them? Well, here is another church, whose preacher never was celebrated for the soundness of his "views"—who, indeed, never paid very much attention to his "views;" but who tried to do something—tried to introduce a new life into his church and into the community in which he lived. What is there about this man that draws the crowd to him? He is not so intellectual as his neighbor; he is not so good a scholar as his neighbor; he cannot write so fine a sermon as his neighbor, but he draws a church full of people. The young flock to him; his Sunday school is the largest to be found for many miles around him, and his church is recognized as a thing of power and progress. This man has reached the hearts of his people, through the sympathies of his poetic nature. He has touched them where they live—not where they think. He has melted them, moulded them, moved them. I tell you, sir, that thin churches are very much attributable to thin ministers—not thin in brains, or scholarship, but thin in heart and thin in human sympathy and thin in spirituality—thin where they should be thickest.

You, Dr. Jones, and your brethren of the pulpit, very rarely get honestly talked to from the pews, but you could learn a great deal more from them than you imagine, if they would talk to you honestly. You rarely hear the truth. Your friends praise you, and your enemies shun you. Let me say to you this: that when you preach you preach with such an air of authority, and such an assumption of superiority, and such an apparent lack of sympathy with my weaknesses and trials, that I find myself rising in opposition to you. I think that all those hearts which have not schooled themselves to accept your teachings as they are rendered, are affected as mine is. Do not deceive yourself with the thought that these feelings are the offspring of depravity, for they are no such thing. They are the spirit's protest against your right to teach. Very differently do many other men affect me. Ah! well do I remember one, sleeping now within a few rods of where I write, and waking uncounted miles away beyond the blue ether that draws the veil between my eyes and heaven, who took my heart in his hand whenever it pleased him. He had an intellect as bright and keen and strong as yours, but his power was not in that. He preached more a sermon that a tasteful scholar would call brilliant, but his power was not in the brilliancy of his sermons. His power was in his sanctified, spiritualized humanity, that never blamed but always pitied me, that took me in its charitable arms and blessed me, that held my hand and gave me loving fellowship, that unselfishly poured out its life that the life of all humanity might be raised to a higher level. You are too great in your own estimation. You are too much impressed with your own dignity. He was Humility's personification, and carried a sense of his unworthiness as a constant burden. Ah! my friend, have you not learned that the weak do not commit their burdens to the strong? Learn of your children, then, who seek for refuge in their mother's slender arms and not in yours.

I told you at the outset that I had no expectation of reforming you, because it is not in you to be reformed. You lack the insight to apprehend spiritual things; you are harsh; you are coarse; you dwell in forms and phrases; you are constitutionally imperious; you are not sympathetic; you are not tempted as other men are. This lack of sympathy in your nature has cut you off from participation in the severest trials and struggles that ever visit the Christian soul. You cannot have charity for others. But there are some who will read this letter and gather perhaps a valuable hint from it. It will not have been written in vain if one preacher learns that his power and usefulness in the pulpit do not reside either in the orthodoxy or the heterodoxy of his "views," do not reside in any system of theology or in any intellectual power, but do reside in a spiritual life, which, acting through its sympathies, by apprehension of and application to human need, nourishes, elevates and spiritualizes human character.

THE ELEVENTH LETTER.

To Stephen Girard Jones.

CONCERNING THE BEST WAY OF SPENDING HIS MONEY.

THE art least understood in this country, where money is made easily and quickly, is that of spending it wisely and well. Most men think that if they could make money they would run the risk of spending it properly; and these same men criticise their fortunate neighbors; yet it is doubtless true that the poor do not monopolize the wisdom of the world, and that if they were to change places with the rich money would be no better spent than it is now. There are enough poor men who succeed, from time to time, in getting rich, to show that wealth rarely brings with it the wisdom which will dispense it with comfort and credit to its possessor and with genuine benefit to the world. Of how few men of wealth can it be said that they spend their money well! One is niggardly, another is lavish; one runs into sports and debaucheries, another into extravagance in equipage; one apes the fashionable, or does what he can to buy social position, another separates himself from others by using his money to thrust his personal eccentricities before the public; one expends thousands in ostentatious charities, and there is occasionally one who impoverishes himself and his family by his improvident beneficence. Caprice and impulse seem to govern the spending of money more than principle, with the large majority of those who have money to spend.

It is a good sign for a man who has made money to take to spending it in any way that is not vicious. It usually shows that he is getting over the excitement of pursuit—that the pleasures of seeking wealth are beginning to pall, and that his heart is looking for a fresh delight. It seems to me to be a good sign, I say, for a man to reach this point, for it proves that he is not a miser. When a man can content himself with a never-ending search for wealth, or rather, when a rich man can be content with the pleasure of adding to wealth which he can never use, and which will be most likely to damage his children, it is evident that he possesses a very sordid nature, or that his character has been made sordid by his absorbing pursuit of gain. To begin to dispense with one hand what the other has gained, and still may be gaining, is to assume a healthy attitude. A man who does this is not spoiling.

It happens in this country, where estates are not entailed, that there are but a few families which, for any considerable number of generations, remain rich. Wealth, when left to voluntary management, is almost uniformly dissipated in two or three generations, so that the great-grandchild nearly always is obliged to begin just where the great-grandfather did. Oftener than otherwise, the reach of a fortune is briefer than this. It is thus that men are not bred to the management and the expenditure of wealth. Our rich men are men who have made their money—men who have spent their youth in learning how to make it, and spent the strength of their years in making it. On becoming rich, they find that there is one part of their education which has been neglected, viz.: that which relates to the best methods of spending money. They are not misers; they are not sordid men; they would gladly do something which shall prove to the world that they are not altogether ungrateful for the handsome way in which it has treated them. Moreover, there is a call within them for repayment in comfort or some form of satisfaction for the toil and care which it has cost them to win wealth. Many a man on reaching wealth has found himself confronted by the great problem of his life, and many a man, unable to solve it, has given up the thought of spending, and gone back to money-getting to seek his sole satisfaction in the excitement of the pursuit. Not unfrequently the process of getting money has been so absorbing, and has so shut out of the mind all culture and all generous pleasure, that the spending of money can fulfil no want.

I have said thus much generally on this subject, my friend, that you may attach sufficient importance to what I have to say to you. You have been fortunate in business. Your enterprise and industry have been abundantly rewarded. All your adventures have been prospered, and you are to-day the richest of all the Joneses. What are you going to do with your money? You have arrived at the point when this inquiry has, I am sure, profound interest for you. You are not a man who can be content with the life-long task of acquisition. You wish to give an expression to your wealth, for your personal satisfaction, and for the purpose of adding privileges to the lot of those whom you love.

In laying out your plans for spending money, the first consideration is safety for yourself and your family. Any plan which contemplates idleness or dissipation for yourself or your children, is illegitimate, and will prove to be ruinous. I am not afraid that you will ever become idle, or, even, that you will become devoted to any form of vicious indulgence. Your habits of industry and sobriety are well formed, and I do not think that you are in any personal danger. The danger relates entirely to your family. You had a hard time when you were a boy, and through all your early manhood worked severely. You have frequently said to your friends that you did not intend that your children should be subjected to as much hardship as you had been. There is danger that your parental tenderness will injure these children. Permit me to ask what harm those early hardships of yours inflicted upon you? Was it not by the means of these hardships that you learned to achieve your successes? Then why do you so tenderly deprecate hardships for your children? Let me warn you that through this tenderness for your children your wealth may become—nay, is quite likely to become—a curse to them.

This notion that wealth brings immunity from industry is the ruin of thousands every year. I do not intend to convey the idea that your children shall all work in the same way that you have done, but that neither girl nor boy of yours shall ever receive the impression that she or he can live reputably or happily without the systematic and useful employment of their minds, or their hands, or both. Give them all a better education than you had, and subject them to the same rigid rules of labor and discipline which are applied to their poorer classmates. Above all things teach them that they must rely upon themselves for their position in the world, and that all children are mean-spirited and contemptible who base their respectability on the wealth of their father. Give all your boys a business, and assist them in it sparingly, and with great discrimination. Let no son of yours "lie down" on you, but make all the help you give them depend upon their personal worthiness to receive it. Money won without effort is little prized, and you may be sure that you will get few thanks from your children for releasing them from the necessity of industry. Nobody knows better than you how necessary industry is to the comfort and pleasure of living, and it should be your special care, in all your schemes for spending money upon your family, that these schemes should involve family employment or improvement. Better a thousand times throw your money into the river, than permit it to spoil your children.

There is danger also to the community in which you live, and to the humble men by whom you are surrounded, in indiscreet benefactions. You are impulsive; your money now comes to you easily; and it is not hard for you to toss a gratuity to those whom you know will be glad to receive it. Universal observation proves that money which does not cost anything is rarely well spent. Men will thank you profusely for the dollar which you give them for some insignificant service, but that dollar is pretty certain to be spent upon their vices, and to help to make them beggars and flunkies. You, doubtless, find yourself surrounded by men who would "sponge" you gladly —who think and say that you could give them any amount of money "and never feel it." It is possible that there are a few mean-spirited Joneses who are already wondering whether you intend to leave them any money, or who have already asked you for "assistance." Never dismiss an application for help without examination; but be careful how you give money to those who are able to earn it. Never think it a disgrace to be thought mean and niggardly by those who wish to get your money, without rendering an equivalent for it.

It is not necessary for me to tell you that no subscription paper ever starts within five miles of you that does not come to you before it completes its round. Now do not get sick of the sight of these petitions. The offices of charity are never complete, and public spirit will always find work to do in fresh measures of improvement. It is right that you, who have been so abundantly prospered, should be abundantly charitable. It is right that you, who have so large a stake in public order and general prosperity, should minister generously to public improvement. The real danger with you, is, that you will give in such a way as to relieve others of the burden of duty which they should carry. This, I confess, is not the common weakness of rich men, but it would be their common error if the community were to have its will. There is a contemptible spirit pervading the social body which would gladly shirk the cost of supporting public charities and public institutions and public improvements and throw it upon rich men. You are the member of a church; and I am ashamed to say that there is quite a general feeling among the members that you could pay the entire expenses "without feeling it." I suppose you might do this without suffering very much pecuniary inconvenience from it; but if you were to do it, it would damage not only the church but you. The jealousy of the very men who would gladly shirk expenses that they would load upon your shoulders, would destroy the harmony of the church and drive you from it. It will sometimes fall to your lot to pay that which niggardly souls refuse to pay, after the willing ones have exhausted their ability. Stand squarely up to this work, like the noble man you are. Never let it be seen by the community that you have any desire to avoid expenditures which it belongs to you to make. Do your part scrupulously. Let every man see and feel that while you will not relieve others of burdens which belong to them, you are determined to carry all which belong to you, to the last ounce. Let society feel that it can rely upon you at all times for that measure of help which it belongs to you to render.

I am aware that I have told you but little as yet as to the proper way of spending money, but I have narrowed the field of inquiry. I have told you never to spend it in such a way as to destroy the industrious habits of your family or to feed the vices of the poor men around you, or to foster a mendicant spirit among your relatives, or to relieve general society from the burdens which should be equitably distributed among its constituents. And now, let me go further and say that all ostentation is vulgar. It is quite the habit of men who become rich to show off their wealth by building large and costly houses, and furnishing them at great expense, and displaying luxurious equipage. The men who do this are very rarely those who have lived in fine houses, or had practical acquaintance with luxurious domestic appointments; but this seems to be the only way in which they can give expression to their wealth. It is, I admit, better than nothing. Streets and building sites are improved by it; upholsterers are benefited by it; various tradesmen are enriched by it; but, after all, ostentation is vulgar, and, moreover, it is not to your liking at all. I know you would not enjoy a splendid house; but you would enjoy a better one than you are in now—therefore, build it. You have good common sense and very little taste; therefore with only general directions, pass this business into the hands of the best architect your money can secure. Buy good taste, and simply insist on convenience and solidity. Build a house which will be in good taste a hundred years hence, so that it may be delighted in by your children and your grandchildren.

It may seem impertinent to tell a man who has been shrewd enough to make money that he is not shrewd enough to spend it, but unless you have good advice, at every step of your progress, in starting an establishment—that is, in building your house, furnishing it, laying out your grounds, &c., &c.,—you will be sure to excite the ridicule of your friends, and bring mortification to yourself. It is quite the habit of men who have made money to grow self-sufficient, and to suppose that because they have succeeded so well in one department of effort, they are equal to any. A practiced eye can tell these men always, by the barren spots and the uncultivated and unoccupied spots which their management betrays. There will always be something to show that the establishment belongs to the man, and that the man does not belong to the establishment—something to show by its incompleteness the incompleteness of the owner's education—a library without books, a palace without pictures, a garden without flowers or fruits, luxury without comfort, or some thing of the sort. You can have such a place as this very easily, by simply taking the whole matter into your own hands, and assuming that you know all that it is necessary to know at starting; but far better will it be for you, and far more for your credit, to assume nothing—to assume that you know nothing, and to look upon the building and equipment of an establishment as a course of education.

I can imagine nothing more delightful or more useful in family life than the two or three years of study and development which attend the proper building of a house, and the appointment of the details of a generous establishment. If you and your wife and your sons and your daughters, beginning with the assumption that you know nothing of the subject, devote yourselves to study and conversation on domestic architecture, and landscape gardening, and furniture and books and pictures, seeking for information and suggestions from every source, you will be surprised and delighted to find in the end that you have entered into a new life. You will find that you have grown quite as rapidly as your house has grown, and that your grounds and gardens have been developed no more than your mind. You will learn, in short, how to spend money upon yourself and yours, in a way which ministers to your growth, your industry, and your happiness. You are the pupils of the artists and scholars and artisans whom you employ, studying under the most favorable circumstances; and you will find that an education thus pleasantly inaugurated may be pursued for life. It may be pursued in books, in society, in travel.

There is much that I might say on this subject of spending money as it relates to other people, in different circumstances, but I am addressing you—a good type of "our successful men." You will find that a costly table will give you the gout, and your children the dyspepsia. Therefore live plainly. You will find that luxurious clothing only ministers to the vanity of your children; therefore insist that it shall be simply good and chaste and tasteful. You will find that your personal necessities are limited, and that, unless you permit your wealth to produce a brood of artificial wants, you can neither expend your money upon your children nor yourself. Have an eye to those around you. The greatest kindness you can show to the poor is to give them employment, and to pay them for it well and promptly. No matter if you do not really need their service. If they need your money, make a service for them. Above all things, do not give them money, unless calamity overtake them, or they become unable to labor. I cannot too strongly insist that in all your dealings with society, with the poor, and with your children, you shall never depreciate in their minds the value of money. Never permit yourself, by your way of spending or bestowing money, to convey the idea that money has cost you nothing; for money is sacred. It is the price of the labor of mind and body, and by some person, at some time, somewhere, was dug from the ground, or drawn from the sea. Because you have been fortunate in accumulating it, you have no right so to spend it as to convey to the public an incorrect idea of its cost and true value.

After all, I imagine that you will find it very difficult to spend well that with which Providence has favored you, in your home life, and in the ordinary charities which appeal to you. In closing, will you permit me to suggest that there is a class of charities and a class of public objects which make special appeal to you. The great majority of your fellow-citizens—even those who possess what we denominate a competence, —have nothing left to pay, after defraying the expenses of their individual and home life, and contributing their portion to the support of society and the ordinary charities. For a great hospital, for a literary or a religious institution, for a public library, for a public gallery of art, they have nothing. These things exist through the contributions of such men as you, or they do not exist at all. They are costly, and must be bought by men of superabundant wealth. You are a rational man, my friend, and know that already you have more wealth than you and your family can advantageously spend. You know, also, that it is always best for a man to be his own executor. If you propose to do anything for the world, do it now. See to the expenditure of your own money, and reap the satisfaction of seeing your generation enjoying the fruit of your benefactions. This waiting until death to give away useless money is the height of folly. The money is yours to spend: spend it, and thus multiply the sources of your satisfaction. Do not wait until you are dead to do a deed from which you have the right to draw pleasure. Make what you can out of your life, and get what satisfaction you can out of your money. There are many chances that it will be wasted or misapplied if you leave it to be administered after you shall have passed away.

THE TWELFTH LETTER.

To Noel Jones.

CONCERNING HIS OPINION THAT HE KNOWS PRETTY MUCH EVERYTHING.

I CANNOT tell whether you believe you know as much as you pretend to know, or whether you assume to know everything as a matter of policy. I am simply aware that there is no subject presented to you in practical science, in art, in philosophy, in morals, in religion, in politics, in literature, in society, upon which you do not assume to entertain a valuable opinion, and that you pretend to be competent to direct every affair, and guide and control every interest with which you have anything to do. It seems to be a matter of principle with you to follow no man's lead, and to refuse to admit for a moment that any man's lead except your own can be worthy of following. I never knew you to ask advice of anybody. It has always seemed as if you regard such a measure as an exhibition of weakness—one which would compromise your position, and bring you to personal disgrace. No: you are authority on all subjects, an expert in all arts, an adept in all affairs; and I do not know of a position for whose duties you would admit yourself to be incompetent, from that of a milliner to that of a minister.

In all my dealings with the world I have noticed that the wisest men make the smallest pretensions. The prominent characteristic of all really great men is teachableness—readiness to learn of everybody, respect for the opinions of others, and modesty touching their own attainments. Sir Isaac Newton was so far from being a vain or pretentious man that he had the humblest estimate of his own knowledge. Baron Humboldt was as simple and unpretending as a child. There are men among the living in this country—the mention of whose names is not necessary to call up their faces—whose exceeding simplicity is only equalled by their exceeding wisdom. My friend, a pretentious man is, by token of his pretentiousness, a charlatan, always. A man needs only to be wise to have learned that no man in the world monopolizes its wisdom, and that there is no man living who cannot teach him something. Human faculty and human life are hardly sufficient for learning one thing thoroughly. Each man pursues his specialty, learning something of it while he lives; and though he may gather much in general touching the specialties of others, he gets little knowledge of detail out of his own walk.

You ought to have seen enough of the world to know that it is full of larger men than you are, or can ever hope to be. You ought to know enough of these men, by this time, to understand that no pretension of yours can raise you to their altitude, or bring you into communion with them. The true position for you, and for me, and for everybody—wise or simple—is that of a learner. Many years ago, as a young physician was standing by the bedside of a sick little child in the dirty hovel of one who was very poor, he was asked by a coarse-looking Irish woman who had come in to do a neighborly office, and was standing at the opposite side of the bed, whether he thought the patient that lay gasping between them would live. He replied that he did not think he could live until the next morning. There was a shrewd twinkle in her black eyes and a positive tone in her voice as she expressed an opposite opinion, and, at the same time, gave her reasons for it. He went away, and thought about it; and the more he thought the more he became convinced that this ignorant Irish woman had been a better student of disease than he had, and that her observation of previous cases must have been both intimate and extensive. He gave to her reasons their scientific significance, and before he reached his office he had become prepared to meet what he had supposed to be a dying patient a convalescent the next morning. He did find the patient a convalescent, and left him, at last, with a valuable addition to his knowledge of symptoms, beyond what books and his own observation had ever taught him. He learned a second lesson by this incident quite as valuable to him, personally, as the first. It was, never to regard as valueless the opinions of the ignorant when they were based on observation, until he had given them a fair and thorough investigation.

This ignorant woman had a right to her opinion. She had earned it, for she had studied. She may have known nothing else particularly worth knowing, but this golden bit of wisdom she had won, and the professors and teachers of medicine everywhere would have honored themselves by humbly learning it of her. Every great and wise brain that lives bows to and honors the humblest hand that brings it food and inspiration; but the position which you assume is an insult to all the humble life—not to say high life—by which you are surrounded. There are one or two things—perhaps half a dozen—which you know better than others. Upon these, men come to you for information; but they know that of all others about which you pretend to know so much you really know nothing.

Let your neighbors estimate you. They recognize you as their superior in one or two points, only. Be thankful that there are one or two things which you really know, and which you can offer in exchange for the world of knowledge which the multitudinous life around you has found and proved. You have your specialties, and other men have theirs; and they know, and you ought to know and practically to acknowledge, that every man you meet has just as much advantage over you as you have over him. It is the habit to speak sneeringly of the poverty of human knowledge, but human knowledge is not poor in the aggregate. It is the individual man that knows so little; mankind knows much. Every secret of the earth and the air and every treasure of human experience is in some man's keeping. If every man could bring to a common depository his special discovery, and the results of his particular thinking and working, and there were a mind large enough to comprehend and systematize the mass, with a life sufficiently long for the enterprise, it would be found that human knowledge is as great as humanity itself. Those little books of wisdom contained in the minds of your humble neighbors, my friend, are open to you, and you owe it to yourself and them to read them with reverence.

I have said that the prominent characteristic of all really great and wise men is teachableness. I may add to this that without teachableness there can be no true greatness, for greatness consists, not in great powers alone, and not in genius alone, but in the power to appropriate, and in the deed of appropriating, the wisdom made ready for it by other minds. For a great man, a thousand minds are thinking, a thousand hands are working, a thousand lives are living; and the results of all this thinking and working and living come to him and pass into his life, contributing to his growth and feeding his power. The canal that crosses an empire, and feeds the roots of a score of springing cities, and gives passage to the bread of a continent, and swells the revenues of a state, has its unseen and unacknowledged feeders, that collect its waters among the mountains, and pour them into its trailing volume, and keep it always full. A great man lays every mind with which he comes into contact under tribute. Great listeners are such men—absorbent of every drop of common sense and even the faintest spray of human experience. Unerring ears have they, to distinguish between the true and the false in the coins that are tossed upon their counter. Finding a man who has successfully pursued some specialty in knowledge or art, they suck his mind as they would suck an orange, throwing away cells and seeds, and drinking the juice for nutriment and refreshment. Do you not see, my friend, that it is not the policy of such men as these to be pretentious? They could not afford it, even were they disposed to be.

The man who takes your position must necessarily go through life at a disadvantage. Your policy drives men from you. Pretentiousness is always and everywhere an insult to society. You repel the knowledge that naturally flows to one who pretends to nothing. Nobody goes to you with a suggestion, because your attitude repels suggestions. You assume to possess all the knowledge that you need. All that you learn outside of the specialty which absorbs the most of your active power, you are obliged to learn by book, or by some trick of indirection. You think that you can only appear to be wise by assuming to be wise; and it is possible that you are right. It is possible that you impose upon a few who would otherwise hold you for a very common sort of person; but all the reputation for wisdom you may secure, can never compensate for what you lose by cutting off these voluntary supplies. Water flows naturally into the humble, open spaces; it never seeks the mountains, except to run around them. Self love, self conceit, pride of opinion—all these are barriers to knowledge and barriers to success. During your brief life, you have suffered from many grave mistakes, which, had you been a teachable man, might easily have been avoided. Your position repelled all information voluntarily offered, and your pride forbade

8*

you to seek for it at the only available sources. You have blundered through experiments whose results could have been given you by a dozen of your neighbors, who took a secret satisfaction in witnessing your expensive failures. He is the wise man only who, holding himself unselfishly tributary to the lives of others, lays hold of, and appropriates, the wisdom won by the life around him. It should be in life as it is in science. If I read the record of a series of experiments by which a certain scientific result is arrived at, I do not feel myself humbled by the discovery, nor humbled by using the discovery for my own advantage. I contribute freely to my own work—I appropriate freely the results of the work of others, as a member of the great commonwealth of life. It is a noble thing to teach; it is a blessed thing to learn.

I have told you that there are probably one or two things about which you know more than others, and touching which your opinions are more valuable than those of others. These things your talents have given you special power to learn; and circumstances have conspired to give you sufficient opportunity. There are ten thousand things on which you assume to have an opinion which you never can have a valuable opinion upon. You have not those peculiar gifts which will enable you to acquire experimental knowledge of them. You pretend to know something of finance, for instance, but it is not in you to comprehend finance. No matter how much you may run against the business world—the whole of your financial wisdom will consist of familiarity with common business forms, and the grasp of the general fact that if a man spends more than he earns he loses money, while if he earns more than he spends, he is making it. You pretend to possess a good literary judgment and taste, but you may study from this time until doomsday and you will never, working by yourself, win either. A life of study with relation to some arts will not win for you what the instincts of some men will teach them in a moment. You have your special knowledge. Talent and opportunity have given it to you. There is an indefinitely large range of life in which you can never discover anything that will be of the slightest value to you or to others. There is an indefinitely large range of life through which you must be led by other minds, or you will never explore them at all. The bird-fancier with whom I walk in the fields is a humble person. I may talk of literature, or art, or science, or politics, and he will show no sign of interest or intelligence; but if I talk of birds he becomes my teacher—nay, for the time, a king. The air around him is full of creatures whose habits and characteristics he knows. He can pour out to me a tide of beautiful knowledge, for the acquirement of which nature has given him the needed eyes and ears and apprehensions. He knows the note of every bird, the nest of every bird, the plumage of every bird. He has possessed himself of their secrets, so that, imitating their language, and taking the advantage over them which reason gives him, he can entrap them. No uncommon bird, be it never so small, can invade his neighborhood without his detecting it; and he marks the retirement of a family from the region that they have frequented as if they belonged to his own species, and had advertised their departure. Now this man's knowledge may be humble, but it is genuine; and it is knowledge which, without his help, you could not have acquired. Nay, you never would have thought of studying birds any more than you would the insects that slide up and down the sunbeams before your door.

Knowledge is a very precious possession, and always dignifies its possessor. The theorists of all ages have filled the world with words, and the pulpit and the library and the school are thronged with words that represent more or less of the material and the spiritual worlds, but knowledge does not come from the pulpit, or the library, or the school. To know a thing is to live a thing—is to come into personal contact and acquaintance with a thing through the use of powers adapted to win acquaintance by contact. I have seen grave doctors and literary men and clergymen and shrewd business men listen for hours to the talk of a man who knew nothing but the habits of a horse, and the means of making that animal the kind and healthy servant of man; and although he could not construct a sentence of English elegantly, they listened as intently as if he were reciting the choicest poem in the language with the unction of a Kemble, forgetful alike of his provincial pronunciation and his incorrect English. These men were learners. They had found a man who knew something. He had been studying the horse all his life for them—studying the horse in the stable; and they were drinking in that which they felt to be positive knowledge. It was worth more than all the books on that subject they had ever read, and worth more than all their observation, because they had not the proper powers for studying the horse by contact. It is thus that every man is studying something for every other man—gaining absolute knowledge by contact with special departments of material existence, or by demonstrating spiritual truth in personal experience.

If you really imagine that you know so much that you do not need to seek advice or ask for knowledge at the hand of even the humblest man with whom you are thrown into relation, you must change your opinion and your policy. You really know but very little, and you cannot obtain any great addition to your positive knowledge without laying those under tribute whose knowledge has been won as yours has been won. Or if you imagine that you have powers adapted to discovery and demonstration in all the varied fields of knowledge, you must relieve yourself of that mistake. You have not even the powers necessary to make a bird-catcher or a horse-tamer. It is not in you to be either; and when you fancy that you could be a speaker of Congress, or a writer for the press, or a preacher, or a secretary of the treasury, if you only had the opportunity for the development or the trial of your powers, you are simply permitting your self-conceit to befool you. You thirst for all the honors, and would be king. Be content with your specialty, and bear me witness that even the bird-fancier and the horse-tamer have dignity and honor which you have hardly won in the higher field in which Providence has placed you, and to which your powers are specially adapted. Conquer your specialty, and take gratefully from other hands the knowledge and wisdom which you have neither the time nor the power to acquire.

You do not know, I suppose, that your assumption makes all who are around you uncomfortable. You do not give them their places. You permit to them no prerogatives and no specialties. The very mother who bore you is not permitted to select her own dress, and the wife that endures you has her milliner and mantua-maker prescribed to her. You are presumptuous enough to believe that you know how to dress a woman. Such presumption stuns me. I tremble when I think how some women—gentle, albeit, as lambs, in the enjoyment of money and liberty—would spurn the dictation of "the humble person who writes these lines," if such dictation should invade the sanctities of their wardrobe. Oh, Noel Jones! You and I know nothing about these things. Our opinion is not good for anything on these subjects. I never bought but one silk on my own responsibility, and the shout of derision with which it was greeted by one inconsiderate member of the family, and the mingled pity and contempt expressed by the silence of the remainder, have remained so terribly fresh in my memory that I have never since presumed to take such a liberty. I meekly carried it back, and begged the smirking clerk to take it again, promising to trade it out in some other way. And the women were right, as they usually are. What did I know about a woman's dress? What did I know about colors that were "trying to the complexion," and colors that harmonized with each other, and colors and fabrics that harmonized with certain ages and seasons, and colors and fabrics that harmonized with other colors and fabrics that for economical reasons were to be worn with them? Nothing; yet it is my private opinion that I knew as much as you do. The truth is that the amount of instinct contained in a woman's little finger is worth more as a guide in all matters pertaining to the female dress than your wisdom and mine combined. Suppose the women should undertake to dictate trousers to us! I would not wear a garment thus selected, on principle; but you—I think such an evidence of presumption on the part of a woman would kill you outright.

No, Mr. Noel Jones, you do not know pretty much everything. Indeed, you know but a very few things thoroughly, and you would now know a great deal more than you do if you had never pretended to know anything. All sensible people measure you. They give you credit for being an ordinarily acute and wise man—the greatest drawback on your reputation being your assumption of knowledge that you do not possess, while the only bar to your popularity resides in your unwillingness to give to men and women the place and consideration to which their specialties of talent and knowledge entitle them.

THE THIRTEENTH LETTER.

To Rufus Choate Jones, Lawyer.

CONCERNING THE DUTIES AND DANGERS OF HIS PROFESSION.

YOU have recently commenced the practice of a profession of which I possess no intimate knowledge. I know, generally, that it is a respectable profession, which requires in those who successfully pursue it the best style of intellectual power, thorough industry, and a vast amount of special learning. I know that it is a profession which, in times of peace, attracts to itself the most ambitious young men, because it affords the best opportunities for rising to positions of influence and power. I know also, that, while it is prostituted to the basest uses—as any profession may be—it fulfils a want in the establishment of justice between man and man, and occupies a legitimate and an important place in society. I can very honestly congratulate you on your connection with this profession, and your prospects in it. Will you read what an outsider has to say of its dangers and duties?

The principal—perhaps the only—dangers which lie in your way relate to your personal character. I regard you as a Christian young man, and I find you in a profession which necessarily brings you into contact with the meanest and the vilest elements in the community. Almost every day of your life you find yourself in communication with men whose motives are vile and whose characters are base. You are obliged to associate with them. You not unfrequently find your interest and sympathies engaged in their behalf. Almost the whole education of the court-room—to say nothing of the office—is an education in the ways of sin. It is there that murder and robbery and adultery and swindling and cruelty and all the forms of crime and vice are exposed, to their minutest details, and as a lawyer, you are necessarily absorbed by these details. There is not a form of vice with which you are not bound to become familiar. All the meannesses and all the rottennesses of human nature and human character, and all the modes of their exhibition, must come into contact with you, and leave their mark. How this can be done without the blunting of your sensibilities I do not know. How this can be done without damaging, if not destroying, your moral sense, is beyond my comprehension. I have heard very good lawyers talk about the most shocking cases in a shockingly professional way, and witnessed their amusement with the details of some beastly case that had found its way into the court-room. I should be sorry to think that you could ever acquire such moral indifference, yet I know that you may, and believe that you will, if you do not guard yourself particularly against it.

It seems to me quite impossible that a man should have a professional interest in the details of a case of crime without losing something of the moral repugnance with which the case would naturally inspire him. I suppose that this loss of moral sensibility may not necessarily be accompanied by actual depravity, yet it is, nevertheless, an evil, for it destroys one of the barriers to depravity. Any influence which familiarizes the mind with sin and crime to such an extent that sin and crime cease to fill the soul with horror or disgust, is much to be deprecated. If you had a young son or a young daughter, you would regard any event which would bring their minds into familiarity with crime as a calamity. It would probably be a greater calamity to them than to you, but why it should be different in kind, I cannot tell. I think you have only to look around you, among your own profession, to find men who have received incurable damage through their professional intimacy with sin. You know numbers of lawyers who take an interest which is anything but professional in the details of a case of shame that ought to fill them with an abhorrence so deep that they would gladly fly from it.

Again, constant familiarity with the weak and the erring side of human nature destroys respect for human nature itself. The more you learn of the members of the legal profession, the more you will learn that great numbers of them have ceased to respect human nature. This seems to me to be one of the greatest calamities that can befal any man. I do not wonder at this effect at all. There is no class of people in the world that see so great cause to hold human nature in contempt as the legal. They come into contact with men whom the world calls honorable and good, and find in them such traits of meanness, and such hypocrisy and dishonor, and such readiness to be crippled under temptation, and such untruthfulness under the pressure of selfish interest, that they naturally enough conclude that one man is about as bad as another, and that no man is to be relied upon where his appetites or his selfish interests are concerned. I say that I do not wonder at this, but it is much to be deprecated; and I know of no way to avoid it, except by free association with good men and innocent women and children. When a man has lost his respect for human nature, he has lost, necessarily, his respect for himself, for, whether he wills it or not, he goes with his kind.

But there is another danger still which will assail you—more subtle and more damaging than professional interest in crime or professional intimacy with the worst side of human nature, and this is professional interest in criminals themselves. I am sorry to say it, but you will find yourself the professional defender of men whom you know to be the foes of society—of thieves, pickpockets, gamblers, murderers, seducers, swindlers. You will find yourself either lying or tempted to lie in order to shield from justice men whom you know ought to be punished. You will find yourself arrayed against law and order, against the peace of the commonwealth, against the purity of society, against morals and religion, in the defense of a man whom you know to be guilty of the crime charged against him, and deserving of the punishment attached to it by the laws of the land. I say "you," because I suppose you will naturally follow in the track of the principal members of your profession. Every criminal is defended to the uttermost by men who are zealous in their attempt to prove him innocent, and to shield him from punishment. Great professional reputations are sometimes acquired by saving from the gallows a man whom everybody is morally certain ought to be hung. A triumph of crime like this is quoted admiringly by the profession, and regarded with complacent triumph by the professional victor. I have heard men talk by the hour to prove that to be true which they and everybody else knew, in all moral certainty, to be false, and to demonstrate the innocence of a man whom they knew to be guilty. Indeed, this mode of proceeding has become a part of the machinery of the law, and is recognized as entirely legitimate. We hear, occasionally, of cases so bad that the counsel engaged in the defence throw them up in disgust; but these are very rare, and I doubt whether such a surrender is regarded as a fair thing by the profession.

Now I ask you, before professional usage has had time to warp your common sense, what must be the effect upon the mind of an advocate, of throwing the entire sum of his personal power—all his logic, all his learning, all his sympathies and desires, all his interests and all his earnestness—into the defence of a man whom he has good reason to believe is a foe to law and order, and justly deserving of punishment for a breach of both? What must be the effect of identifying his own personal and professional reputation with the success of a criminal, in his attempt to shield himself from justice? What must be the effect upon his mind of a triumph over the law for himself and for him who has trampled it under his feet? I know that there is a specious style of argument in use in your profession which takes the decision of a case out of the hands of a criminal's professional defender, and gives it to the jury before which he is to be tried. The lawyers will say that an advocate has no right to decide on the guilt of a man on trial—that his work is to defend; and that twelve men, whose business under the law it is, will make the decision. This is strictly professional talk—the talk of men who make a distinction between law and justice—the talk of men who stand by that which is simply legal, and let justice and right take care of themselves. These men would tell you that if you were engaged in the defence of a person whom you were morally certain was guilty of the crime charged upon him, you would not be excusable did you not do what you could to save him, by a resort to every legal trick and quibble of which you might be the master. This is precisely what they do. They personally rejoice in the defeat of justice. Whenever justice is defeated, and right denied or destroyed, in "a court of justice," there is always present one lawyer to rejoice personally over the fact—a lawyer whose sympathies and success are identified with the triumph of the wrong-doer.

I remember, when a lad, of witnessing an interview between a couple of eminent lawyers,—each of whom has come to great personal and political honor since then,—which to my unsophisticated moral sense, was quite shocking. One had been attending a term of court in an adjoining county, for the management of an important case in which both were interested. The returning lawyer greeted his associate with a triumphant flourish of his riding stick, and exclaimed—"We've beaten them! we've beaten them!" Thereupon they gleefully talked the matter over. It seemed very strange to me that they could rejoice at having "beaten them," without the slightest reference to the matter of justice and of right. If the man had been engaged in a personal fight or a horse race, and had come off the winner, he would have expressed his triumph in the same way, and with just as little reference to the moral aspects and relations of the case. This was a professional triumph, and it did not matter, apparently, whether justice had shared the victory with him, or had been vanquished with his opponents in the suit. This professional indifference to justice and to right, acquired by the identification of your own personal success with the safety and success of those whom you know or believe to be criminals, is what I warn you against. I tell you that this cannot be indulged in without injury to you, and were it not an ungrateful and offensive task, I could refer you to illustrious instances of legal depravity, induced by earnest defence of the wrong. I could point you to eminent lawyers, with whom lying is as easy as breathing—men who do not scruple to misrepresent, misconstrue, prevaricate, cheat, resort to all mean and unworthy subterfuges, suppress, make use of all available means to carry a point against law and good society and pure morals, in favor of ruffians who deserve nothing better than the halter or the prison. A lawyer has only to do this thing to a sufficient extent with sufficient earnestness, to lose both his sense of, and respect for, the right, and to become morally worthless.

I suppose that you will tell me that I am a dreamer, and that I am suggesting something that is entirely impracticable, when I advise you never to permit yourself to be professionally arrayed against justice. Your seniors in the profession will smile contemptuously at my suggestion, I know, and I will not blame them, for I know how fatally they have been warped by their practice. I take the broad ground that no man, whatever may be his profession, has a moral right to defeat, or to strive by all the means at his command, to defeat the ends of justice in the community in which he lives, and that no man can consciously identify himself with the wrong, and fight earnestly for its triumph, without inflicting incalculable damage upon his own moral sense and moral character. I do not believe that you—a professional man—have a moral right to do in a court of justice what I—not a professional man—have no moral right to do. I do not believe that you have a moral right to stand up before a jury, and try to mislead it by tricks of language, by quibbles of law, by springing of false issues, by engaging their sympathies at the expense of their reason, and I know it is a moral impossibility for you to do it without damage to yourself. Mark my words: I do not advise you to leave a client while you have a reasonable doubt of his guilt, or a case where you have a reasonable doubt of its injustice; but I say without hesitation that when you become convinced that you can go no further in the professional advocacy of a man or a cause, without arraying yourself against right, against justice, against the well being of society, you are bound, in duty to God, the state, and yourself, to abandon that man or cause; and all the professional sophistry which you and your professional brethren can muster can never convince me to the contrary.

The fact that the money of thieves and scoundrels will buy the best legal service to be had is notorious, and it is but a short time ago that it appeared in evidence, in a court of justice, that a certain crime was committed by a man who, calculating his chances for detection, relied upon a certain lawyer to "get him off." Was that lawyer practically a friend or a foe to society? Had he a right professionally, or in any way, so to conduct himself as to encourage the commission of crime?

But I leave this point for one closely related to it. The whole tendency of your profession, as it seems to me, is the substitution of a human for a divine rule of action. I think that a lawyer naturally comes to view every action and every man from a legal stand-point. All your practical dealing with men is on a legal basis. If there be a hole in the law, large enough to let through your criminal client, you will pull him through. A flaw in an indictment will spoil a case legally, while morally and rationally it is not touched at all. You feel justified in doing anything that is legal, to favor your client, or your cause. Your conscience has come to identify that which is legal with that which is right. The law of the Lord is perfect; the law of man is imperfect; and your constant association with the latter, naturally crowds the other out of sight. You measure the actions of men by that prescriptive red tape of yours, and the standard of right within your own soul is degraded.

Litigation is one of the evils of the world, and is voluntarily pursued more to secure personal will than sound justice. There are many cases of doubt in which a suit at law is entirely justifiable, not to say desirable; but you are already old enough to know that two-thirds of the civil cases tried would never find their way into court if simple justice were all that the litigants were after. Selfish interest, personal greed, pride of purpose, wilfulness and waywardness—these are the elements of litigation everywhere. Now it is the misfortune of your profession that its revenue is very largely dependent upon the selfishness and stubbornness of men. It is apparently for the personal interest of every lawyer to foster a litigious spirit in the community, and to nurse every cause of difference between men. That this is done by the more disreputable of your profession, I presume you will admit; and I am sure that you will not deny that the better class of lawyers do not discourage litigation as much as they might. My friend, here is a duty which I exhort you not to avoid. If you can prevent a lawsuit between citizens, in which no important end of justice is involved, or settle a difference which is more a question of personal will than of right, then, as a Christian man, and a good citizen, you are bound to interfere at whatever personal sacrifice. If I were to foster a legal quarrel between neighbors, which my advice would prevent, you would call me a bad neighbor and a bad citizen. The fact that it is for your professional interest that neighbors quarrel does not relieve you from the same opprobrium, for the same mean office. There is no man in the world so well situated for promoting the ends of peace between citizens as the lawyer, and if he do not avail himself of his opportunities, then he fails in the offices of good citizenship.

I hesitate to speak of one of the dangers to which you are exposed, because it supposes that you can cease to be a gentleman; but you will find that, in the court-room, lawyers not unfrequently indulge in practices which, while they may be strictly legal, are not gentlemanly. I declare to you that I have witnessed more cowardly insolence in a court-room than in any other place that pretended to be controlled by the laws of decency. I have seen men whose years and positions should have given them dignity, brow-beat and badger and, in every way sufferable by a too indulgent court, abuse old, simple-hearted men and honest women, whose crime it was to be summoned as unwilling witnesses by the party opposing them. I am not familiar with bar-rooms or brothels, but I think it would be hard to find in any of them such flagrant instances of ill-breeding as are witnessed at every term of court in every court-room in the land. I do not care how high the lawyer stands who takes advantage of his position to abuse the honest witnesses which the law places in his hands for examination:—he is no gentleman. He is a mean and cowardly scoundrel. Under the protection of the court, he indulges in practices so insulting to honest and blamelesss men and women that all there is within them of manhood and womanhood rises to resent the indignity, yet they are powerless, and the unwhipped coward rubs his hands over his clever boorishness and brutality. For your own sake—nay, for decency's sake—be a gentleman in the court-room, and do what you can to compel others to be gentlemen. This gratuitous abuse of those who are so unfortunate as to be summoned as witnesses, by the lawyers into whose hands they fall, is the shame and disgrace of your profession.

Rather a formidable array of dangers you will say, I imagine; and perhaps you will add that it is not a very promising display of duties. I grant it, but I seek the glory of your profession and the good of yourself. The profession of the law, when it confines itself to the ministry of justice, is one of the noblest in which a man can engage. In that aspect, it is worthy of the devotion of the best minds which the country produces; but the profession of the law when it is used in the prostitution of justice for hire,—when it is freely lent, with all the personal resources of him who practises it, to aid the notorious criminal to escape the punishment due to his crimes, and to thwart the adjustment of the right between man and man, is an outrageous nuisance. I would have you remain what I believe you now are—a Christian lawyer—a man who can never forget that the royal right is above the legal letter—that God lives, and claims a place in the human soul, and that He refuses to live there side by side with venal falsehood. I would have you retain, amid all the temptations of your profession, your love of justice and of right, and your hatred of injustice and wrong. I would have you guard yourself against confounding that which is right with that which is legal, so that the latter shall always seem essentially the former. I would have you maintain in all places the demeanor of a gentleman. I would have you a good citizen and not a promoter of litigation. I would have you so pure, and upright, and honorable, and peace-loving, that men shall refer their differences to you rather than carry them into court. I do not wish to appeal to any selfish motives, but my opinion is that such a lawyer as I desire you to be, would command a premium in all the markets of the world.

THE FOURTEENTH LETTER.

To Mrs. Royal Purple Jones,

CONCERNING HER ABSORBING DEVOTION TO HER OWN PERSON.

I HAVE a great respect for the human body. As a piece of vitalized mechanism it is the most admirable thing in the world. As the dwelling-place and associate and minister of the human soul—the possessor of those exquisite senses through which that soul feeds and breathes and receives knowledge and inspiration—its first home—the vestibule of its immortality—I give it honor. It is a thing of dignity—a sacred thing—sacred to its possessor, and sacred to those to whom in sacred love it may be given. Whenever the soul rises to a true appreciation of its own worth, it pays honor to the body which bears it. Barbarism wanders in negligent nakedness, but civilization, of whatever type, honors the body—covers it from sight

—drapes and protects it with reference to ideas of comfort and taste. Innocence, like that possessed by infancy, may feel no shame without drapery, but virtue, a very different thing, grows crimson when uncovered.

The human body is a thing of beauty as well as of dignity. All civilized nations have recognized this fact, and all have striven, more or less effectually, to reveal or enhance that beauty by dress. It costs almost as much to clothe civilization as it does to feed it; and human ingenuity is taxed to its utmost, and all departments of nature are laid under tribute, to produce the fabrics witn which civilization enrobes itself.

This domain of dress is one which Fashion has conquered and made peculiarly her own, and it ought to be a matter of interest to you, madam, as I doubt not it will be to people generally, to note how far that power has sophisticated the idea of personal dignity on which dress is based. Up to a certain point of beauty of fabric and elaborateness of ornamentation, dress can be carried legitimately, and with no violence to personal dignity; but beyond that point, there must always come a resort to the barbaric idea, which must necessarily bring personal degradation. Barbarism, without any thought of personal dignity—of bodily sacredness—has gratified its vanity and desire for distinction by means of marks and gaudy ornaments. It has tattooed its skin, hung rings in its nose, worn beads on its neck—at its girdle—at its knees, stuck feathers in its hair, and daubed paint upon its face. This kind of ornamentation—an exhibition of personal vanity—is the highest expression of the highest idea which barbarism has ever entertained concerning the human body. This vanity touching the person, that feels gratification in ornaments and trappings, has not the slightest natural connection with that better idea which finds in graceful drapery the refuge and shield of the dignity belonging to the living tenement of the living soul. You will see, therefore, that whenever fashion carries dress to extremes, or beyond the point of giving the body a graceful and becoming covering, it always resorts to barbarism to help it out—to partial nakedness, or to jewels and precious stones and trinkets and ribbons and laces and all possible sorts of ornaments. The fashionable belle of Newport and Saratoga enters the assembly room or the dining hall only to show that she is sister of the South Sea Islander, and that the same idea controls them both.

The curse of Eden seems to have been the subjection of the soul to the service of the body. When I reflect upon the relative dignity and importance of the soul and the body—the immortality of the one and the mortality of the other, the heavenly alliances of the one and the earthly alliances of the other, the Godlike capacities of the one and the brutal appetites of the other—it astonishes me to realize that the soul's work in this world is, in the majority of cases, simply that of procuring food and raiment and shelter for the body. It astonishes me to realize that under every form of civilization the body is the soul's tyrant and leads it by the nose. Naturally, the body is uppermost in the general thought. Men must have food and clothing and shelter, or die; they must win all these for their children, or lose them. So, under the circumstances of our life, and the usages of our civilization, the body is necessarily a constant topic of thought. It is not strange, therefore, that the soul often forgets that it is master, and loses sight of its own dignity and destiny in its habitual devotion to the satisfaction of bodily want.

But this, Mrs. Royal Purple Jones, is not your trouble. You are not obliged to work for a living. Your money has been earned for you by other hands, and your devotion to your body is voluntary and not compulsory. Your soul, with all its fine capacities, and its possibilities of culture and of goodness, is the willing and devoted slave of the body in which it lives. Your person is the central motive of your life. Now that I call your attention to the fact, will you tell me, or attempt to realize to yourself, how much thought and how much time you devote to the hair that adorns your head? How much of both do you give to the little matter of eye-brows?—how much to your teeth?—how much to your face as a whole, with all the considerations of cuticular texture and complexion?—how much to your hands?—how much to your arms?—how much to your neck?—how much to your feet?—how much to your general configuration? Madam, you are in love with your own body, and the keenest delight of your whole life consists in having that body admired and praised. The sense of personal modesty and dignity which flies to dress for refuge has really no place in you. I do not mean that you are an immodest woman, but that this sense of personal sacredness has been overcome by personal vanity so far that you dress rather to show than to hide your body—to attract attention to your person than to make it the modest and inconspicuous tenement of your soul. What is it that most absorbs your time? What is it that most absorbs your money? Is it not dress? Think of the silks that you buy, and the study that you bestow upon their selection and manufacture into garments! Think of the hats and the gloves and the jewelry, and of the intense and absorbing interest which attend their purchase and first wearing! Think of your constant observation and criticism of the dress of your friends! I believe you will admit to yourself, if not to me, that I have found you out—that I know where you have your life.

When you attend a party, what is the highest object you contemplate? Do you attend for the purpose of enjoying the conversation of dear friends, or to minister to the pleasure of others by your own gifts of conversation, or to enjoy the sight of pleasant faces, or to hear music, or to engage in dancing, or such other amusements as may be indulged in? Is it for all or any of these that you attend? Is it not rather to show your dress, and to display, for the admiration of the gentlemen, and the envy of the ladies like yourself, your richly draped and elaborately ornamented person? Would you have a single motive to attend a party if you were obliged to dress inconspicuously and plainly? Is it not true that your one absorbing thought with relation to such attendance concerns the dressing and adornment of your person? And when you return from it, do you think of anything except the simple questions as to how you looked, and how you compared or contrasted with certain other women who unfortunately are as much devoted to their persons as you are? When you walk in the streets, what are you thinking about? Are you thinking of what you see in the shop-windows, or what the shop-windows see on you? Are you not conscious that many eyes are turned upon you to see what you take great pains to make attractive to all eyes? When you dress for church, and when you enter the sacred edifice, what thought is uppermost in your mind? Is it a thought which becomes the holy place, or is it still of the drapery and the ornaments with which you have hung your person? Are you not filled everywhere—under all circumstances—with these same vanities? Do they not haunt and hold you constantly?

You need not blush and hang your head, because you find that I know you better than you have hitherto known yourself, for you have plenty of company. The whole world of fashionable women is controlled by the same thoughts and ideas that control you—a world of women who, in the pursuit of personal adornment, have adopted the ideas of barbarism, and have personally descended toward barbarism through such adoption. You, madam, and all of your associates, have, in your devotion to the dressing and bedizening of your persons, degraded yourselves pitifully. The whole number of fashionable female souls are but slaves to the fading bodies in which they live. When I look in upon a fashionable watering-place, and see how dress and personal adornment absolutely monopolize the time and the thought of the fashionable women assembled there—when I witness the rivalry among them—the attempts to outshine each other in diamonds and all the tributaries to costly dress—when I see their jealousies, and hear their ill-natured criticisms of each other, and then realize that these women are mothers and those of whom mothers will be made, I have opened to me a gulf of barbarous selfishness—a scene of gilded meanness and misery—from which I shrink back heart-sick and disgusted. Good Heaven, madam! what and who are you? Are you all body and no soul? Is it decent business for a decent soul to be constantly engaged—absorbingly occupied—in ornamenting and showing off for the gratification of personal vanity the body it inhabits? Do you realize how low you are fallen? Do you realize that you are come to the small and indecent business of getting up your person to be looked at, admired, praised,—that the most grateful satisfactions of your life are found in this business, and that the business itself is but a single moral remove from prostitution?

If I have succeeded in picturing you to yourself, perhaps you will be prepared to follow me into a contemplation of a few of the natural consequences of your infatuation upon your character and happiness. Will you look among your fashionable female acquaintances, and find one who is making any intellectual progress? The thing is impossible. There is nothing more conducive to mental growth and development in devotion to the keeping and dressing of the person of a woman, than there is in the keeping and the grooming and harnessing of a pet horse. Look at a man who devotes himself to a horse. He may be a very pleasant fellow, and ordinarily intelligent, but if he is enamored of his animal, and gives himself up to his care and exhibition, becoming what is known as a "horse man," that ends his intellectual development. When horse gets highest in any man's mind, culture ceases. Now, madam, it would make no difference, practically, whether you were devoted to the person of a horse, or the person of a pet dog, or the person of Mrs. Royal Purple Jones. The mind that engages in no higher business, or that finds its highest delight in no higher pursuit than that of grooming and displaying a beautiful body, can make no progress into a nobler life. Practically you will find this the case everywhere. You will find that your fashionable friends do not grow at all. They move along in the same old ruts, prate of the same old vanities, go the same old rounds of frivolity, and only become less sprightly and agreeable as the years pass by. Just what you see in these people, madam, I see in you.

There is another very sad result which comes naturally from this devotion to your own person. You are already grown supremely selfish. You have permitted your personal vanity to control you so long that you can really see nothing in the universe but yourself. It seems proper and right that everybody should serve you. Any labor that would soil or enlarge your small white hands—any toil that would tax the powers of your petted body—any service for others that would draw you away from service to your own person—is shunned. Your mother, your sisters, your friends, are all laid under tribute to you, and your petulance under denial has made them your slaves. Absorbed by these thoughts of yourself, devoted to nothing but yourself, making room for no plans which do not relate to yourself, you have come to regard yourself as the world's pivotal centre. It does not occur to you at all that the kind people around you can have any interests or plans of their own to look after. All the fish must come to your net, or you are unhappy; and if those around you are not made unhappy it is not because you do not try to make them so. Sometimes you act like a miserable, spoiled baby, and then, under the spur of jealousy, you act like an infuriated brute. The tendency to this shameful selfishness is natural and irresistible, in all who devote themselves, as you have done, to the care and exhibition of their persons. Others may cover it from sight more than you do, by a more cunning art, but it is there. It cannot be otherwise, and I cannot conceive of a type of selfishness more nearly perfect than that which the character of almost any fashionable woman illustrates.

There is still another result which naturally flows

from supreme devotion to the person, viz: vulgarity. Madam, I look anywhere in God's world for genuine refinement and lady-like instincts and manners rather than to fashionable society. True refinement and gentle manners can never find their home in any society in which selfishness reigns. True refinement has brains. True refinement has a heart. True refinement always makes room in the world for others. True refinement has consideration for others. True refinement does not find its satisfactions in the display and adornment of the body. True refinement refuses to be governed by fashion, having within itself a higher and a purer law. True refinement shrinks from conspicuity and show. True refinement engages in no unworthy and unwomanly rivalries. You know that the coarsest words you ever hear from the lips of women—the harshest, meanest, worst things—the lowest expressions—you hear from the lips of those of your own set. Yet mark the impudent hypocrisy of the thing. You and your set assume to be the leaders of society—the ton—the pattern women of the nation—so far refined that all other women are counted vulgar! My friend, (if you are not by this time become my enemy,) how can you help becoming vulgar when you have been nothing for years but your own groom? How can you help becoming low when you have thought of nothing for years but your own person?

You are vulgar. All your pursuits are vulgar. Your rivals and associates are vulgar, and your ambitions are as vulgar as those of the horse-jockey.

I would not be misunderstood. I admire a well dressed woman. I admire a beautiful woman, and I thoroughly approve all legitimate efforts to render the person both of man and woman agreeable. Men and women owe it to their own dignity to drape their persons becomingly and well, and they can do this without acquiring an absorbing passion for dress, or giving any more than the necessary amount of thought and time to it. The fact is that a woman who is what a woman should be has no need of elaborate personal ornament to make her attractive. A pure, true heart, a self-forgetful spirit, an innocent delight in innocent society, a wish and an effort to please, ready ministry to the wants of others, graceful accomplishments willingly used, sprightliness and intelligence, these are passports to personal power. Relying upon these, there is no woman whose person is simply and becomingly dressed who is not well dressed. With any or all of these, the person becomes pleasing.

As I write, there comes to my memory the person of a woman whom everybody loved and admired—the most thoroughly popular woman I ever knew. She was welcomed alike in fashionable and refined society, and behaved herself alike in both. She was not beautiful, but she was charming. She never ornamented her person, but she was always well dressed. A simple, well-fitted gown, and hair tastefully disposed, were all one could see of any effort to make her person pleasing, and these seemed to be forgotten, and, I believe, were forgotten, the moment she entered society. When friends were around her she had no thought but of them—no desire but to give and receive pleasure. If she was asked to sing she sang, and, if it ministered to the pleasure of others, she sang patiently, even to weariness. She was as intelligent and stimulating in sober conversation as she was playful in spirit, and though she loved general society, and mingled freely in it, not a breath of slander ever sullied her name, and not an emotion was ever excited by her that did not do her honor. Every man admired and honored her, and every woman—a much greater marvel—spoke in her praise. Many a belle, dressed at the height of fashion, entered her presence only to become insignificant. Diamonds were forgotten and splendid dress was unmentioned, while her sweet presence, her self-forgetful devotion to the pleasure of others, and her gentle manners, were recalled and dwelt upon with unalloyed delight.

Madam, I have been painting from life. I have painted you from life, and I have painted this friend from life—a friend so modest and so unconscious of her charms that she would weep with her sense of unworthiness if she were told that I had attempted to paint her. How does the contrast strike you? Do you not see that you are a slave and that she is a free woman? Do you not see that she has entered into the eternal realities of things, and that you are engrossed in ephemeral nothingnesses? Do you not see that she is a refined woman and that you are a coarse one? Do you not see that her unselfish devotion to the happiness of others is beautiful, that her unconsciousness of her charms is beautiful, that her simplicity is beautiful, and that your selfishness and your devotion to dress and your jealousy and your rivalries are all vulgar and ugly and hateful?

It is complained of by many of your sex that men regard woman as only a plaything—a creature to be humored and petted and controlled, and indulged in as a troublesome luxury. It is complained of that woman does not have her place as man's equal—as his friend, companion, and partner. Are men entirely in the blame for this opinion, to the limited extent in which it is held? Suppose men were to take you and such as are like you as the subjects of their study: what would be their conclusions? Suppose they were thoroughly to comprehend your devotion to your own person,—to realize the absolute absorption of all your energies and all your time by the frivolous and mean objects that inthrall you—what would be their decision? What does your husband think about it? Excuse me for mentioning him, madam. I am aware that he occupies a very small share of your attention, but, really, the man who finds you in money has a right to an opinion upon this point. You do not care what his opinion is? I thought so. You have ceased to love him, and he has ceased to oppose you. It is impossible for your husband to love you. It is impossible for any man either to love or to honor a woman so selfish as you are; and your sex may blame you and those who are like you for all the contempt which a certain class of men feel for women. You degrade yourself to the position of a showy creature, good for nothing but to spend money. You teach men contempt for your sex, and it is only the modest and intelligent women whom you despise that redeem it to admiration and love.

THE FIFTEENTH LETTER.

To Miss Felicia Hemans Jones.

CONCERNING HER STRONG DESIRE TO BECOME AN AUTHORESS.

WILL you permit me to reply publicly to the private letter in which you have informed me of your strong desire to engage in literary labor, as a form of self-expression which embraces all your ambition and all your wish to do good? Had yours been the first letter of the kind that had reached my hand, I should not have ventured to treat your case publicly; but I have received a hundred such, and many of these came to me so reluctantly—after such a struggle with inclination—that I am convinced that you are only one of a class which numbers its thousands in every part of the country. Indeed, the world is full of women whose unsatisfied lives and whose overflowing natures fill them with suggestions of ideal good, to be won in some field of art. If these women could use the pencil or the chisel, many of them would be artists, or would try to be artists; but the pen is the only instrument of expression with which their fingers are familiar, and they come to regard it as their only resort. I have a deep sympathy with this desire to write, and I am sure that you will receive what I have to say to you as the words of a friend.

You have a strong desire to write, you tell me. Well, this desire to write may be associated with the power to succeed as a writer, or it may not. The desire to write is not even *prima facie* evidence of fitness for writing. This desire, as I have already intimated to you, is quite universal. One of the strangest anomalies of human nature is exhibited in the general desire to do those things which are the most difficult to do. A little man desires to do the work of a large man, and a large man desires to be thought nimble. A man of slender limb desires to be an athlete. It is very common for men to have a strong desire to sing or to play upon a musical instrument who could not sing or play with a century's practice, because they have neither voice nor ear. I suppose that nine out of ten of the students in our colleges have a strong desire to be orators, and you know how much, or how little, the desire amounts to. Most probably the student who has the least desire to be an orator of any one in his class is the one who is most certain to become one; and perhaps you will readily see that he who is conscious of possessing the orator's native power has least occasion to desire it. Of the great multitude who write, you know that only a few succeed. Nine out of every ten fail—perhaps even a larger proportion than this. A very few of these fail, doubtless, through no real fault of their own, but through unfavorable circumstances; while the most of them find to their mortification and their cost that their desire to write misled them entirely with regard to the work which nature intended them to do. So you see that I do not think much of desire as a guide to one's work in the world. Indeed, I think it the most unreliable index ever consulted.

I think I understand the process through which your mind is constantly passing. You take up a book, from the pen of a favorite author, and you are refreshed and nourished and inspired by it. You are exalted by this communion with a highly vitalized and fruitful mind, and feel yourself longing for action and expression of some kind. It is the most natural thing in the world for you to desire, before everything else, to be a writer. You admire the author who has inspired you. You imagine that the mind that has within it the power to work such marvels upon you must be a supremely happy mind. His position of power seems very enviable to you,—if not enviable, very desirable. The results of his efforts upon you are so good and so wonderful that it seems to you as if it must be a glorious thing to work them. You long to do for others what he has done for you. You long to be regarded with love and admiration as an inspirer. This is the same feeling that is excited in a sensitive mind by public speakers. Thousands of very commonplace men are excited by oratorical efforts in the pulpit and on the platform, to a strong desire to become public speakers. The desire to be preachers, or orators, or lecturers, or public debaters, is always excited in some minds by listening to the different varieties of public speaking, yet the most of these need only to try once to become convinced that desire is a very poor index to power.

This desire to write is intimately connected with—perhaps it is one of the expressions of—the longing natural to every heart to be recognized. The heart that loves men, and is conscious of the wish and the power to bless them, longs for the recognition of men. All of us who are good for anything have this longing. We long for the recognition of our real value; we long for a place in the respect and the love of those around us. It is not unfrequently true that those whose affections have been unsatisfied at home—whose plans of domestic life have miscarried—or who are immediately surrounded by those who will not, or who cannot sympathize with them—who are every day associated with those by whom they are undervalued—turn to the public for that which has been denied them at home. I do not know whether I hit your case in these remarks or not, but I should think it strange if I did not. It is not common for a woman who is satisfied in her affections, who is surrounded by sympathetic friends, and who holds a good position securely, to care for, or even to think of recognition beyond. On the other hand, it is very common for women whose domestic surroundings and society are not satisfying to look to other fields for recognition, and to none so commonly as to that of authorship.

In your letter to me, you speak of your wish to do good by writing. I do not question the sincerity of this wish. It may flow from the benevolence of your nature, developed by Christian culture, or it may have been inspired by the consciousness of good received from the writings of others. But you must remember that one's motives may be very good while one's native gifts may be but poorly adapted to literary effort. Your motives decide nothing as to your power. That you may readily see, by looking at the pulpit, filled by men whose motives are excellent, while the power of one half of them has never found demonstration, and never will. I have sometimes thought that there were no preachers in the field who more uniformly have the noblest motives and the most charming Christian spirit than those who have not the slightest power in the pulpit. No person should write without good motives, but good motives alone never made a good book. Goodish books are written in great numbers by people who write with good motives and incompetent brains, but I suppose you do not care to write such books as these.

I have made these remarks, not to prove to you that you are incompetent to write a book, and not for the purpose of making you believe that you are incompetent. I have made them for the simple purpose of showing you that your strong desire to write, even when backed by the purest and most benevolent motives, is no evidence that you can succeed. The world is full of the desire to do good and great things, and it is not lacking in worthy motives. You are not peculiar in these things. You share them to a greater extent than you suspect with your neighbors. You would probably be astonished to learn how many there are among your immediate friends who have been moved by the same desires that move you, yet you may be able to see that not one of them could succeed as a writer. There may be one among your friends, too, who has not had any desires about the matter, but who has written by a sort of natural necessity, without recognition or publication. What do you think of such a man as Theodore Winthrop, who wrote quite a little library of books that could find no publisher until he was killed, and that have now made him famous? Such a man writes because it is a necessity of his nature to write, and I venture to say that he never sought advice on the subject. He certainly was not checked in production because the publishers would not print his books, and the public could not read them. Still, it is possible that you have just the native gifts that would command success in authorship, though I wish you to feel that the probabilities are against you, and to open your eyes to these probabilities.

We will suppose that you have those native gifts which, under favorable conditions, would enable you to succeed, and we shall still have these conditions to look after. The first of these is the possession of something of genuine value to communicate. Your power of expression may be unsurpassed, and your style may be exceedingly attractive, but unless you have something of value to convey, these will avail you nothing. What have you of knowledge or wisdom to give to mankind? How much have you thought and felt and lived? How much more have you thought and felt and lived than those for whom you wish to write? Do you, in your character and in the general results of your life, stand so far above the mass of mind around you, as to be able to inspire it and to lead it to higher ground? This question has a great deal more to do with your success in authorship than that which relates to the desire to write. This touches the vitalities of the matter. Have you knowledge which the world has not, and which the world needs? Has your life led you through such paths of experience and observation that you feel qualified to lead or direct others?

Another essential condition to success in authorship is time. To write a brief poem, or a clever little essay for a magazine or a newspaper, it does not require much time. You can do this in the intervals of domestic labor, and it would be rather a help than a hinderance to labor. It would be quite likely to sweeten labor, and give significance to leisure, to have on hand the work of embodying in some good or graceful form some good or graceful thought for other eyes, but this would be playing at authorship. To succeed in a field which numbers among its competitors the brightest and best minds of the world—minds which devote all their time to their work—involves the entire devotion of one's time to the effort. Success in authorship cannot be won without time. The man who gains the ear of the world by the labor of ten years may be accounted fortunate. It is possible that an author may write a book very early in life which will be read, but it will be forgotten within a shorter time than he occupied in writing it. A book lives by its value—by the amount of genuine life, or food for life, which it contains; and it takes time to collect this. Defoe, the author of "Robinson Crusoe," was also the author of more than two hundred other works, and it is more than likely that you never heard of any of his books except this that I have named. Yet this book was among his last. It was written after many years of authorship—the only book of all his life that had vitality enough in it to survive him. It took nearly sixty years of life, and more than thirty years of authorship, to bring him where he could write Robinson Crusoe. Mr. Motley, the now celebrated historian, began early as a novelist, and his book failed so signally that when he emerged from his obscurity as a historian, nobody remembered the novel. Where do you suppose Mr. Motley spent the ten years, more or less, that divided the issues of the novel and the history? He spent them in his study, at his desk, in patient labor, giving to his project the very best years of his life.

Now will you ask yourself whether you have time to give to a life like this? Do you realize how much of sacrifice it involves?—sacrifice of health and society and domestic pleasures? Are your plainly indicated domestic duties such as to permit you to devote yourself to a life like this? Is the time that it would absorb, so entirely at your disposal, through abundance of means for your support, that you could afford to run the risks of authorship? This question of time is a very important one to a person who is poor. A writer may devote one or two years to writing a good book, and then look one or two years for a publisher, for the best books by new authors have notoriously begged for publishers. "Waverley" and "Uncle Tom's Cabin" and "Jane Eyre" were all beggars for publishers. You would not be apt to have a better fate. But suppose, after the usual working and waiting, you were to obtain a publisher. Then he waits for the proper time to bring out your book. It may be three months; it may be a year. Six months after the day of publication he will give you a note for whatever may be due you for copyright, payable in four or six months from its date. Do you think that this is an exaggeration? Every author knows it is not. It is the simple truth, and many of them know that when the day of settlement has come, their copyright has amounted to nothing; or they have found that their note, when they were fortunate enough to get one, has not been paid at maturity, on account of the failure of its maker. A man must be rich and independent or poor and desperate, to afford to write a first book. There are hardly ten persons among the thirty millions of America who rely on the writing of books for a living, and the most of those have a hard task of it. There is but one way in which a person who is dependent upon his labor for a living can write a book, and that is to write it in the intervals of labor, which labor is devoted to the simple purpose of getting a living. You will readily see that a writer thus engaged is at work very disadvantageously.

Another condition of successful writing is patience. A man furnished with all the necessary means of support, and impelled to write by the desire which moves you, and by your wish to do good, will find that, after the labor of a few weeks, the desire dies out. The impulse to write, born of the inspiration of the books which one reads, is very fiery and very fine at the first, but it is hard to stretch it over a period of six months or a year, through weariness, and headache, and confinement, and doubt as to the result, and disgust with the failure to satisfy one's own taste and judgment. The man or the woman who writes on, after the original inspiration has lost its impulse—labors on in the drudgery of detail—in polishing, trimming, rewriting —comes at last to an irksome task, and is only sustained in it by a self-supported determination. A fresh interest will sustain labor, but when a book has been fully constructed in the mind, and realized in the imagination, and nothing remains but the labor of writing a limited amount from day to day for many months, all of which writing must be done before one can get any sympathy from others, it takes a will as patient and unyielding as that which a besieging army needs before a fortress that is to be approached by inches. Do you possess this patience—this persistence—this adamantine will—which will stand and command and do after desire and inspiration are gone, and even the motive of doing good has been discouraged?

I have thus attempted to show you how easily you may be misled as to your abilities by your desires, and what the conditions of successful writing must be, admitting that your abilities are all that you suppose them to be. I have exaggerated nothing, but tried to give you a faithful survey of the ground, so that if you still feel impelled to undertake writing, you may approach your task with a good understanding of its difficulties. If I were intent on discouraging you—if that were my motive at all—I might go further, and speak of what are supposed to be the "satisfactions" of authorship. I might tell you that the article which so inspired you probably left the author a disgusted man. It is more than probable that the books which have pleased and strengthened you most, are, at this very moment, regarded by the writer as unworthy of him, and altogether unworthy of the purpose to which they were addressed. I might tell you of the incompetent criticism, the mean personal attacks, the careless condemnations, and worst of all, the undiscriminating praises which are every successful author's lot. But as you do not propose to write to please yourself, and are actuated solely by the desire to do good, the effort would be irrelevant. It would be very painful to me to feel that I had dissuaded any man or woman from a legitimate career, or to know that I had turned aside any mind from a walk of usefulness; but I cannot but believe that talk like this will save ten from failure for every one whom it will deter from success. There are many men and women who are always unsettled upon this matter. They feel that they suffer hardship from circumstances which prevent them from writing. I cannot but believe that an intelligent survey of the difficulties of authorship, and a comprehension of the fallibility of the signs of power to succeed, usually relied upon, will settle this question forever in their minds. It is one of the curses of life to feel that we are out of place, and to feel that we might be doing something better than that which engages our powers. The world is full of the unsatisfied, multitudes of whom, I believe, turn their eyes to the field of authorship with desire, and with more or less of conviction that there are success and satisfaction in it for them. These people will never write, but they will always be thinking about it; and they need something to turn them back upon their legitimate field for the satisfactions which they seek. I believe this letter will have an influence on your mind, as well as on theirs. Of this, I feel measurably certain: if you were born for an authoress, you will find that within you which will set all my wisdom aside, and push on. There is a consciousness of power and a faith in success which I cannot define, but before which I bow; and if you have these—Heaven imparted—I bid you God speed. But do not, I beg you, mistake a simple desire to write, which you share in common with thousands, for the divine impulse to which I allude.

THE SIXTEENTH LETTER.

To Jehu Jones.

CONCERNING THE CHARACTER AND TENDENCIES OF THE FAST LIFE WHICH HE IS LIVING.

I HAVE been watching you with painful solicitude for the last five years. You were originally what people call a wild boy, with no particular vices, but with strong passions and a great overflow of animal spirits. You came into manhood with a cigar in your mouth and a reputation for "spreeing," in both of which you apparently took a proud delight. You abused every horse that you had the opportunity of driving, and particularly affected a dashing turn-out. You liked the society of sporting men, and took naturally to their ways and their morals. You cut loose from the influence of the Christian friends around you, and broke the Sabbath, and frequented the haunts of vice, and engaged in scenes of dissipation, and laughed at those who yielded themselves to the control of conscience. You are a good-natured person enough, but you are wicked, and while you maintain a place in respectable society, you are regarded with fear by the good and with suspicion by all. It is understood among the women that you are not a pure man, and it is known, by some of them, that you have abused the confidence of more than one. All of your friends have heard sad reports of your sins when beyond their sight, and all regard you as a ruined man.

I wish to call your attention particularly to this point, viz: that the community regard you as a ruined man already. You do not imagine this to be the case, at all. You have no idea that you are ruined, or that you are to be ruined. You are not aware that you have the reputation of being ruined. Now permit me to set you before yourself.

You are not under the control of principle, in the slightest degree. You have some notions of honor, but they are entirely conventional. They would not keep you from breaking your pledge to a woman, or breaking her heart, and I say, therefore, that you have no principle—not even the principle of personal honor which you doubtless suppose you have. There is, thus, nothing to restrain you from the most unscrupulous means for securing your personal ends, and nothing to stand between you and the gratification of your sensual desires, except the law. Now will you not decide for yourself how far a man in this position is from ruin? Do you imagine that you are, to any extent, under the control of principle? Does principle restrain you from indulgence in strong drink? Does principle withhold you from association with lewd women? Does principle forbid your use of the profane oath or the obscene jest? You know it does none of these things. Then why do you fancy that you are controlled by principle? Why do you fancy that there is anything within you to keep you from moral ruin? If you are not ruined to-day, you are pretty certain to be very soon, because salvation involves reformation, at which you scoff.

Let me ask you to look around you, and see what those have come to who began where you have begun. There goes your neighbor with a blotched and burning face and a stuffed skin, whose drink will just as certainly kill him as if it were arsenic. He stood once where you stand to-day. He did not dream, ten years ago, that he was ruined; but he has taken no new step to bring him where he now stands. He only continued to do what he was already doing. There was no principle to stand between him and destruction. He drank with his friends occasionally, then he drank with them habitually, then he drank alone to gratify a thirst which drink had created, and which will never die while his vitiated body lives. Look at that other neighbor of yours, with a dark red skin and a troubled eye, who knows where he is going. It is not ten years since he was not even suspected of drinking, but it came out that he had learned in secret to love hot liquors, and that he had set his heart against reform. That man is in the straight road to hell and he knows it, and you, on the same road, stop at the wayside resorts and drink with him. Delirium tremens waits for that man and is sure of him. Look at that little circle of neighbors younger than those to whom I have called your attention. Do you see how they are changing? Do you not see that they are growing preternaturally heavy, and that they are becoming more habitual in their visits to the dram-shop and in the indulgence in drink at home? Have you any doubt as to where they will be in the course of ten years more?

Having looked at these, suppose you go with me to visit certain others who have arrived at the close of their journey. There sits one in his doorway—a miserable wreck, filled with gouty pains, unable even to taste of the liquor which has destroyed him, and loathing the food which he has no power to digest. There writhes another in torment—in a delirium whose horrors are beyond conception, as they are beyond description. There sits another in the sun, from whom the flesh has all fallen away—who is left feeble and flaccid and foolish—a poor, broken-down, diseased wretch, beyond the reach of help. There sinks another in paralysis, a helpless mass of bloated flesh.

What do you think of these men, Mr. Jehu Jones? Does it seem as if that handsome face and those shapely limbs of yours could ever arrive at such degradation? You have only to keep along in the track which you now follow, with no fears and no compunction of conscience, to pass through the various stages of ruin which these men have presented to you. There is but one end to a life of drink, and that is hell. It matters little whether the popular doctrine of future torment be admitted or not to make my statement good. A body long abused by drink becomes all that we can conceive of as hell. It is the dwelling-place of torment—the home of horror. You see these men on their way to ruin. You know just where they are going, and I see you are going on the same road, to the same end. Tell me whether you do not love drink better to-day that you did five years ago. Tell me whether it does not take more drink to satisfy you than it did five years ago. Tell me whether you are not drinking oftener than you did even two years ago. Tell me whether you do not think of it oftener when away from it than you did one year ago. Tell me whether your conscience reproves you at all, and whether, under the accumulating evidences of your essential ruin, you have felt the smallest alarm as to what may be the result of your indulgence. I see what you do not see—that you have acquired an appetite for liquor. You used to drink it only when on a frolic; now you drink it every day. Now let me tell you what all observation and experience teach—that you will love it more and more as the years pass away, and will be less and less inclined to relinquish its use. Why should I not speak of you then as a ruined man?

There is another element that enters into your ruin. You have, for the past five years, consorted with ruined women. When you were younger, evil companions and evil desires and curiosity led you into their society. There were certain things in that society that disgusted you then. To-day you are at home in it. Sir, you are a beast. You delight in the company of women who shame the names of mother, sister and wife—of prostitutes who sell for gold that which, in God's pure economy, is sacred to love—of women whose touch is pollution and whose hold upon you is damnation. Oh Heaven! When I think of the young life around me that is permitting its feet to be directed into these terrible paths of sin—when I consider how seductive these paths are to youthful appetite and passion—when I remember how opportunity invites from ten thousand hiding-places—and when I realize that there is no vice which so deadens or destroys the moral sense as that of licentiousness, I am sick and almost in despair. You are old in this vice, but there are those around me who are young in it, as you were once—boys, whose feet hang upon the verge of a precipice more fearful than death—young men—with Christian mothers and pure sisters—whose characters are as base as their bodies are diseased. Do you shrink from this vice, and from the society which it involves? Are you not in love with it—so much in love with it that you do not enjoy the society of pure women? Are you not so much in love with it that the society of pure women only brings to you shameful suggestions? And yet, you think you are not ruined! Sir, you are rotten. If mind were subject to the laws of matter, and moral corruption were accompanied by the phenomena which characterize physical decay, you would stink like carrion.

I have no words with which to express my sense of the ruin which this single vice has wrought in you. Men who drink are sometimes reformed, and if they have not proceeded too far in their vice, they come back to a self-respectful manhood. The taint left upon the morals is not so deep that it cannot be eradicated; but a man who has been debauched by licentiousness, is incurable. I do not mean that he cannot reform, but that he must always be weak, and must always carry with him a sense of degradation and shame.

Do you persist in believing that you are not ruined?

There is, of course, one aspect of your case in which you are not. It is possible for you to reform, but you have no idea of reforming. You base no hopes or calculations on reformation. That is why I declare you to be ruined. You voluntarily block up the only way of escape from ruin. If a man, loving your welfare, speaks to you of reformation, you are angry with him. If he ventures to reprove you for your vices, you bid him mind his own business. You brace yourself against every influence which is intended to reform you. You join hands with those who are nearer the grand catastrophe of their lives than yourself. You scoff at temperance and purity in life. You laugh at religion. You glory in your independence of all weak and womanish notions of morals and of life, yet God knows that in these weak and womanish notions of morals and of life abides your only hope of deliverance from a career whose end is certain disaster and misery. Look at the poor women who share your debaucheries. Are they ruined, or are they not? How great a chance does any one of them stand of reformation and a happy life? Can you not see that their lives are morally certain to end in wreck? Do you not know that their steps tend directly into the blackness of darkness—into a horrible tempest of remorse, whose howlings even now ring in their ears in the intervals of artificial madness? What are you better than they? You are not better than they. They are your equals and your companions, travelling the same path—bound to the same perdition.

Would to Heaven I could paint to your imagination the horrors of a lost life, that you and all who may gaze upon the picture might shrink from the gulf, and make haste to reach safer and higher ground! I would call up to your vision your former self—the unpolluted boy and young man—full of life, and joy, and generous impulses, with inclinations drawing you toward sin, and pure influences from parents and home and heaven dissuading you from it. I would show you how, yielding to these better influences, you might now be an honored member of society, with a virtuous wife at your side, and pleasant children at your knee—with a smiling heaven above you, a safe future before you, an approving conscience within you—with conscious freedom from the slavery of thirst and desire—with self-respect, and that strength which comes from the possession of the respect of others. I would show you all your possibilities of excellence in manhood, of virtuous happiness, of self-denying effort for the good of society, of domestic delight, of faith and confidence in a great and glorious future. And having shown you all these, I would show you all those—lost. I would show you a life that might have been that of an angel thrown away—its physical health and resources wasted in debauch eries—its mind feasting only on impure imaginations, and delighting only in impure society—its heart reeking with corruption—its pure ambition dead—its present controlled by animal appetites, rendered foul by indulgence and fierce by their feverish food, and its future overclouded by fear. I would show you a man —the noblest being God has placed upon the earth—thrown away—transformed into a beast—a gross, unreasoning thing, that glories in its appetites, and boasts of their indulgence—a being lost to decency, to self-respect, to happiness, to good society, to God—lost even to the poor inheritance of conscious shame.

A lost life! What is it? Theologians stickle about words in describing the future of the vicious, but if any theologian can tell me how a man can live the life of a beast, subjecting his soul, with all its pure aspirations and inspirations, to the service of lust, and throw away his life in this miserable perversion, and be able to look back upon it from the other side of the dark river with anything but remorse, he will explain to me the strangest anomaly of the moral universe. Sir, the thing is impossible. A lost life is something that belongs to a lost soul. What is in store for such a soul, of possible reform in the long ages which lie before it, I cannot tell. I only know that it has lost its best chance, and, so far as I know, its only chance, for everlasting happiness. I only know that such a soul must go before its Maker a polluted thing, full of regret for its life of folly and of sin, consciously out of harmony with all pure and heavenly society, shorn by the death of its body of every source of pleasure. I know that you are losing your life—that you are marching straight into the jaws of physical and spiritual destruction. You refuse to reform. You scoff at reform. What remains? A life—lost! My God! What a surrender of thy gift is this!

It would be a gratification to me, sweeter than any material success, to turn your feet into the path of virtue; but I have not much faith in so happy a result of this expostulation. For many years I have watched the career of such men as you. Death has reaped a dozen crops of them within my short memory. The young men who occupied ten years ago the position which you occupy to-day, are nearly all of them dead. One remains, here and there, a played-out man, whom circumstances have restrained from going on to absolute suicide. The rest have hidden their faces in the grave, and no one speaks of them except as of men who lost their lives. Look back, yourself, and see how many of those with whom you have joined in carousal and debauchery are now dead. They are scattered all along the track of your dissipated life. How many of your companions have reformed? Can you name one? I hope you can name many, but if you can, you are more fortunate than I am. No, sir, I have but little hope of saving you, though it would give me more joy than it would be possible for me to express to be able so to present to you your situation as to frighten you back from the precipice which you are rapidly approaching. If any entreaty of mine could save you, I would willingly get on my knees before you, and beg you to save yourself by immediate reform. I would do anything to arrest your progress to destruction, and I would do anything to turn the feet of those who are younger than you away from the life which you are leading.

I have written you this public letter mainly to arrest the attention and secure the salvation of those who are tempted as you were, when younger, to forsake the path of temperance and purity. It is more than likely that when you commence this letter, and notice its drift, you will lay it down without reading it. It is more than likely that many young men who are not fallen, but who are liable to fall, will read the whole of it. It is mainly for the use and the warning of these men, that I have drawn your picture, and I place it before them with hopefulness of a good result. I would show them by your life whither license leads. I would show them by your loss what illicit indulgence costs. I would warn them by the disasters and death of your friends to abstain from the intoxicating cup, and to shun the house of her whose steps take hold on hell. Licentiousness, were it not the vice of all ages, might be called the special vice of this age. Certain it is that never in the history of Puritan America did this vice reap to its infectious bosom such harvests of the young as it is reaping now. Certain it is that this vice never spread its temptations before the public with such impunity as now. The community seems to be benumbed, discouraged by its boldness, strength, and prevalence. It literally advertises itself in the public streets, and no man lifts indignantly his voice against it. Ruin and riot thrive. The dram-shop and the brothel are everywhere, and into either of these no man can go without endangering both his body and his soul. You, Mr. Jehu Jones, will sometime know how precious a possession is in the hands of these young men—know when you would give the world, were it yours, to win back the innocence and health and peace which you will have forever lost—know when you would esteem it a privilege to adjure them to keep their bodies and their souls from the grasp of those appetites which will have borne you into the realm of despair.

THE SEVENTEENTH LETTER.

To Thomas Arnold Jones, Schoolmaster.

CONCERNING THE REQUIREMENTS AND THE TENDENCIES OF HIS PROFESSION.

WHEN I review the life and character of Dr. Thomas Arnold—to honor whom your name was given to you—it is easy for me to understand why he was so great a schoolmaster. He was a profound scholar, surpassing in attainments most of the professional men of his time. He was a rare historian, with a minute knowledge and a philosophical appreciation of modern times, and that mastery of antiquity which enabled him to write a History of Rome that competent critics have characterized as "the best history in the language." He was a theologian of the highest class, paying but little respect to systems constructed by men, but drawing directly from the fountain of all theological knowledge—the Bible. Above all, he was a man—a large-hearted, catholic man—a gentle, loving man—full of ėnthusiasm—devoted to reform—in constant communication with the best minds of his age through a private correspondence, which astonishes all who now look upon its record—a laborious, conscientious, Christian man. Knowing all this of the man, it is not surprising to me that he was the greatest schoolmaster of his generation, or that we cannot find his peer among the schoolmasters of to-day.

I heard some years ago that you had "fitted" yourself "for teaching"—that you proposed to make teaching the business of your life. I know comparatively little about you, personally, but I know what, in the definitions of the day, fitting one's self for teaching means. It is commonly understood that when a man is "fitted for teaching," he is fitted to conduct recitations in the various branches pursued in the ordinary schools, having thoroughly gone through the usual textbooks himself. If a man knows grammar, he is "fitted" to teach grammar. If a man has learned arithmetic and natural philosophy, and astronomy and moral science, as he finds them in the accredited text-books, he is "fitted" to teach all those branches of learning. We hear constantly of young men and women who are "fitting themselves for teaching," and we know exactly what the process is. We hear often of those who travel in foreign parts as a preparation for labor in the pulpit, and in other professions, but I do not remember an instance of travel, undertaken by man or woman, as a preparation for teaching. "Fitness" for teaching seems to consist solely in the ability to conduct recitations, and when this ability is compassed, so that a candidate for the teacher's office is able to pass an examination before a board more or less competent for the service, he is "fitted for teaching."

It is true that teachers fitted in this way for their work are competent to impart what, in the common language of the time, is called "an education." With all that is written intelligently on this subject of education at the present time—and in my judgment the subject is better understood now than it has ever been before—it is astonishing how almost universally it is the opinion that education consists in the cramming into a child's mind the contents of a pile of text-books. I do not think that I exaggerate at all when I say that three quarters of the teachers of American youth practically consider fitness for teaching to consist in the ability to conduct recitations from the usual text-books, and that three quarters of the people who have children to be educated regard education as consisting entirely in acquiring the ability to answer such questions as these teachers may propose from the text-books in their hands. The larger view of teaching and of education is not the prevalent view. Teaching is conducted often by men who are not competent to do anything else. They take up teaching as a preparation for other work. A man teaches as a preparation for preaching —as a stepping stone to something better—as a means of earning money to enable him to learn some other work. "Fitness for teaching" seems to come a long time before fitness for anything else comes, and is certainly not regarded as indicating a very high degree of intellectual advancement.

I have no means of knowing how far I have defined your notions, or your attainments, in these statements, but I have prepared you, certainly, for the proposition that real fitness for teaching only comes with the most varied and generous culture, with the best talents enthusiastically engaged, and the noblest Christian character. Dr. Arnold was a great schoolmaster simply because he was a great man. His "fitness" for hearing recitations was the smallest part of his fitness for teaching. Indeed, it was nothing but what he shared in common with the most indifferent of his assistants at Rugby. His fitness for teaching consisted in his knowledge of human nature and of the world, his pure and lofty aims, his self-denying devotion to the work which employed his time and powers, his lofty example, his strong, generous, magnetic manhood. That which fitted him peculiarly for teaching was precisely that which would have fitted him peculiarly for any other high office in the service of men. His knowledge of the ordinary text-books may not have been greater than that which you possess. His excellence as a teacher did not reside in his eminence as a scholar and a man of science, though that eminence is undisputed; but in that power to lead and inspire—to reinforce and fructify—the young minds that were placed in his care. He filled those minds with noble thoughts. He trained them to labor with right motives for grand ends. He baptized them with his own sweet and strong spirit. He glorified the dull routine of toil by keeping before the toilers the end of their toil—a grand character—that power of manhood of which so noble an example was found in himself.

Now, my friend, how well fitted for teaching are you, tried by the standard which I place before you in the character of Dr. Arnold? I do not ask whether you are as great and good a man as Dr. Arnold. I do not require that you should be as great and good as he; but I ask you whether you now regard, or whether you have ever regarded—save in the most general sense—this matter of fitness for teaching as being anything more than fitness to govern a school, and conduct recitations intelligently? Having acquired this sort of fitness sufficiently to enable you to get a position, are you pushing on in the pursuit of that higher fitness which will give you the power of an inspirer of the youth who are placed in your charge? That is the question most interesting not only to your pupils, but to you. Are you making progress as a man, by constant culture? Are you bringing your mind into communication with other minds, that you may gain vitality and force by contact and collision? Are you reading—studying—striving to lift yourself out of the dead literalism of your recitation-rooms, so that you can win higher ground, whither you may call the young feet that grow weary with plodding? Outgrowing all bondage to forms and technicalities and mere words and names, have you mastered ideas, so that you can give vitality to your teachings? Do these text-books, to the mastery of which you devoted some years, and in the exposition of which you now spend much of your time, still enthrall you with the thought that they hold the secret of an education within their covers; or, standing above them, do you look down upon them as rudimentary, and as things which, in the consummation of an education, are left far behind?

In the course of your own education, you were, as I happen to remember, placed under the tutelage of several different masters. Will you now look back and recall them all, and tell me which of them you remember with the most grateful pleasure? Tell me which of them all did you the most good—which of them left the deepest mark upon your character, and accomplished most in building up and furnishing your mind? Was it the most learned man of them all, or was it the wisest man? Was it he who was most at home in the text-books, or he whose mind was fullest of ideas? I know that you can give but one answer to my question. The answer will be that he who was the most of a man was the best teacher, and the name of that one will always awaken your enthusiasm. You have been peculiarly unfortunate if you have not, at some time in your life, been under a teacher who had the power to inspire you to such an extent that all study became a pleasure to you, and the school-room, with its tasks and competitions and emulations, the happiest spot which the earth held. And now, when you look back to this man, or when you hear his name mentioned, your mind kindles with a new fire, as if you had touched one of the permanent sources of your moral and intellectual life. Your best teacher was the man who aroused you—who gave you high aims and lofty aspirations—who made you think, and taught you to organize into living and useful forms the knowledge which he helped you to win. In short, he was not the man who crammed you, but the man who educated you—who educed those powers in which reside your real manhood.

I wish to impress upon you the great truth that your excellence and success as a teacher depend entirely upon the style and strength of your manhood. The ability to maintain order in a school, and to conduct recitations, with measurable intelligence, is not extraordinary. It is possessed by a large number of quite ordinary people, but that higher power to which I have attempted to direct your attention is extraordinary. The teachers are not many who possess it, or who intelligently aim to win it. It is not a garment to be put on and taken off like a coat, but it is the result of the loving contact of a generous nature with those great and beautiful realities of which the text-books only present us the dry definitions. The greatest naturalist of this country—perhaps the greatest of any country—is a teacher whose equal it would be hard to find among a nation of teachers; and this is true, not because he knows so much, but because he is so much. No young mind can come within the reach of his voice and influence without being touched by his sublime enthusiasm. No pupil ever speaks of him, save with brightened or moistened eyes. I have heard women pronounce his name in many places, scattered between Maine and the Mississippi, and always in such terms of gratitude and praise that it has seemed as if the brightest days which they recalled were not those of childhood, and not those spent with parents, or lovers, or husbands, but those passed at the feet of that noblest of educators and inspirers—Agassiz.

I have already intimated that this question as to what kind of a teacher you are to be is quite as important to yourself as to your pupils. The character of a schoolmaster has been, in the years that are past, notoriously a dry one. It is really sad to see with how little affection many old teachers are regarded by those who were once their pupils. There are men who, having spent twenty-five years of their lives in teaching, are always spoken of by the boys who have been under their charge as "old" somebody or other. "Old Boggs," or "Old Noggs," or "Old Scroggs" has stories told about him, and is never mentioned in terms of respect—much less in terms of affection. Now why is it that these men are remembered so lightly? It is simply because they are teachers, and not men. They are all good scholars enough, but they have not that in their characters and personalities that wins the love and respect of their pupils. I suppose it must be admitted that there is something in the business of teaching which tends to make the character dry. The drudgery and detail of teaching are hardly more interesting than the drudgery and detail of the work of the farm, or of the kitchen. Indeed, I think the work of handling the rake and the hay-fork a more refreshing exercise for the mind and body than that of turning over and over again a verb, or a sum in simple addition, or even a proposition in Euclid. This everlasting handling of materials that have lost their interest is a very depressing process, to a mind capable of higher work; and a mind that can interest itself in such work, and find real satisfaction in it, is necessarily a dry and unlovely one. Do not misunderstand me with regard to this latter statement. A teacher may be interested in his routine of labor through the effect that he aims to work upon the young minds before him, and he should be intensely interested in it; but there is a class of teachers who seem to be really interested in the drudgery of repetition, and these are always dry characters, and they grow dryer and dryer until they die.

You have fitted yourself for teaching, in the usual way. You are prepared, by the mastery of your text-books, to "teach school." The probability is that you will never have any pupils who will be as familiar with these books as yourself, and, so far as maintaining your position is concerned, you will have nothing to do but to handle over and over again familiar and hackneyed materials. Whatever there may be of moral and mental nutriment in these materials, you have already appropriated and digested. There is in them no further growth for you, and, so far as any good to you is concerned, you might as well handle over so many dry sticks. Exactly here is where a multitude of teachers stop. They never take a step in advance. The work of teaching is severe, and when they are through with their daily tasks, they are in no mood for study, or experiment, or intellectual culture in any broad and generous sense. Any mind will starve on such a diet as this, and the work of instruction becomes to such a mind degraded below the position of an intellectual employment. I warn you against the danger of falling into this unfruitful routine, which is certain to dwarf you, and give you a dry and unattractive character. You must make intellectual growth and progress by the means of fresh intellectual food, or you must retrograde.

There is another reason why the business of teaching has a tendency to injure the character. While contact with young and fresh natures tends to soften and beautify character under some circumstances, I doubt whether this influence is much felt by those who are engaged in teaching. We take into our mouths some varieties of fruits as a corrective, which would hardly be regarded as the best of daily food. We take medicines which operate kindly for a brief period, but, if they are continued longer, the system becomes accustomed to them, and they lose their medicinal effect. It is thus with the influence of children. To the literary man, or the man of business, the occasional society of children and youth is very grateful and refreshing, but it soon tires, and if necessarily long continued, becomes irksome. A really vigorous and healthy mind, forced to remain long in contact with the minds of children, turns with a strong appetite toward maturity for stimulus and satisfaction. Now you are obliged to spend the most of your time with children, or those whose minds are immature. You are almost constantly with those who know less than you do, and in this society you will be quite likely to forget—as many schoolmasters have forgotten before you—that you are not the wisest and most learned man in the world. It is under these circumstances that pedants are made, alike conceited and contemptible. To a mature mind, there is no intellectual stimulus in the constant society of the immature, and you are certain to become a dwarfed man if you do not mingle freely in the society of your equals and your superiors. I do not know of a man in the world who, more than the teacher, needs the corrective and refreshing and liberalizing influences of general society and generous culture, to keep him from irreparable damage at the hand of his calling. You must mix with thinking men and women, and you must feed yourself with the products of fruitful lives, in books, or your degeneration is certain; and you will come to be regarded as a dry, pedantic, uninteresting man.

A man or a woman who does nothing but deal out small facts to small minds is certain to become over critical in small things. You have not been a schoolmaster so long as to forget the peculiar emotion once excited in you by the presence of a "school-ma'am." Before this day of larger ideas, to be a school-ma'am was to be a stiff, conceited, formal, critical character, which it was not altogether pleasant for a man to come into contact with. There seemed to be something in the work which these women performed that threw them out of sympathy with the free and easy world around them. They carried all the formal proprieties, all the verbal precisenesses, all the pattern dignities of the school-room, into society; and one could not help feeling that they had lost something of the softness and sweetness and roundness that belong to the unperverted female nature. All this has been improved by the modern correctives, but the reminiscence will help you to comprehend one phase of the danger to which you are exposed. I think that if the world were to give its unbiassed testimony touching this subject, it would say that it has found teachers to be men who give undue importance to small details, and who seem to lose the power to regard and treat the great questions which interest humanity most in a large and liberal way.

And now, before closing, let me do the honor to your position which I find it in my heart to give, for I hold that position second to none. The Christian teacher of a band of children combines the office of the preacher and the parent, and has more to do in shaping the mind and the morals of the community than preacher and parent united. The teacher who spends six hours a day with my child, spends three times as many hours as I do, and twenty-fold more time than my pastor does. I have no words to express my sense of the importance of your office. Still less have I words to express my sense of the importance of having that office filled by men and women of the purest motives, the noblest enthusiasm, the finest culture, the broadest charities, and the most devoted Christian purpose. Why, sir, a teacher should be the strongest and most angelic man that breathes. No man living is intrusted with such precious material. No man living can do so much to set human life to a noble tune. No man living needs higher qualifications for his work. Are you "fitted for teaching?" I do not ask you this question to discourage you, but to stimulate you to an effort at preparation which shall continue as long as you continue to teach.

THE EIGHTEENTH LETTER.

To Mrs. Rosa Hoppin Jones,

CONCERNING HER DISLIKE OF ROUTINE AND HER DESIRE FOR CHANGE AND AMUSEMENT.

YOU, who were Rosa Hoppin, when I first met you—a restless child—have married into the great Jones family, and henceforward, through all time, the blood of the Hoppins will mingle with that of the Joneses. What changes will be wrought by this combination of strange currents does not now appear, though I suspect that they will not be strongly marked. Indeed, I am inclined to believe that there have been Hoppins in the family before, for I find many Joneses who constantly remind me of the Hoppins, and any number of the Hoppins whose ways are suggestive of the Joneses.

The children of the Hoppins do not differ in any essential respect from the children of the Joneses.

Pretty nearly all children are, or might be, Hoppins. They live upon little excitements. They are constantly on the alert for new sources of pleasure. They delight in being away from home, in new and strange places. They are miserable without society and miserable without change. Children have no power of application to the performance of duty, no sources of interest and amusement within themselves—no love of work. They grasp a new toy with eagerness, and tire of it before it is broken. The moment they are compelled to sit down, they seize upon a book, or ask for a story, or whine with discontent. They are unhappy unless something is going on for their amusement, or they are going somewhere, or doing something, with amusement for their special object. The genuine Hoppins rarely outgrow this disposition, but carry it with them to their graves. The Hoppins do not sit down quietly in their houses of an afternoon, unless compelled to do so by circumstances. They are either in the street, or at the house of a neighbor. In the evening, either their houses are full of Hoppins, or they are out visiting Hoppins, or attending some place of amusement, or doing something at home to make them forget that they are at home. Nothing so weighs down the spirit of a Hoppin as home duty, and the confinement which it involves. Children are half-hated because they interfere with indulgence in the passion for going somewhere and doing something pleasant, and husbands become bores when they happen to love home, and love to find there a thrifty and contented home-life.

You—Mrs. Rosa Hoppin Jones—are still a child. You are married, and you have children, but I do not see that you are changed at all. You have the same love of novelty that possessed you when you were a little girl—the same greed for change—the same horror of staying at home—the same fondness for "visiting"—the same restless impatience with work—the same desire for constant and varied amusement. You are fond enough of dress, but dress does not absorb you. You tire of the old dresses it is true, and greet the new ones with genuine pleasure, but, after all, dress is not your passion. Fine dress costs you too much care and trouble, and personal vanity is not your besetting weakness. You would willingly leave all this matter of fine dress to Mrs. Royal Purple Jones and her circle, if you could be permitted to have what you call "a good time." You delight in a party, or a picnic, or an excursion, or a play, or a pageant, or a circus, or an Ethiopian concert, or a frolic of any kind; and you never pass a day at home, even when you have around you the society you love best, without the sense of irksomeness. You will either have your house full of those who destroy all the sweet privacy and communion of home-life, or you will invade the home-life of some other person—Hoppin or otherwise. And yet, madam, I like you. You are not a disagreeable person at all. Your nature is affectionate and pleasant, your tastes are social, you are generous, and pure, and true-hearted—as much so as you were when you were a child. Your husband is fond of you, and proud of you. He has tried to adapt himself to you, and to take delight in that which most interests you; yet I cannot but think that a man who carries his burden of care would delight most in a quiet home, and in the certainty of finding a contented wife in it, whenever he comes back from the work by which he supports it.

There are some women in the world—and you seem to be one of them—who never heartily, and with devoted purpose, enter upon the work of life. You do what you are compelled to do by circumstances. If circumstances should compel you to do nothing, you would do nothing. All work is an interference with your favorite pursuits, or your mode of spending time. Nothing would be more agreeable to you than to have the privileges of going, and gadding, and seeking for fresh amusements all your life. You certainly must recognize a difference between yourself and many estimable women of your acquaintance. You know many women who, from choice, and on their individual responsibility, have undertaken a life-long task to which they cheerfully and systematically devote their powers. They keep their houses, and understand the minutest affairs connected with them. They devote themselves to the right training, in body, mind and morals, of the little ones born of them. In society, they are the reliable ones—the women of character and consideration. They are women who use time for good ends, outside of themselves, and who take delight in action—in the useful employment of their powers. You must, I repeat, recognize a difference between yourself and these women. They have their life in exertion; you have yours in amusement. You exercise no power, but find your sweetest satisfaction in the varied impressions that are made upon your sensibilities.

There is another class of women from whom you must find yourself differing very appreciably. I allude to those whose greatest delight is in opportunities for culture. If you read a book, you read it for the same purpose that a child reads. You read only for amusement. You never read for instruction. The idea of taking up a book for purposes of study, is one that never occurs to you; and you have no delight in a book that taxes your mind. Whatever you read must amuse you—interest you—absorb you—or you lay it down and call it stupid. There is no culture in such reading as this—there is only dissipation. You read a book for the same purpose that you attend a theatre, or engage in a frolic—for the simple purpose of having your emotional nature excited, and your sensibilities played upon. You never seek for mental nourishment or mental exercise anywhere. Thus, though you read a great deal, and really enjoy some works that are enjoyable by sensible people, you gain nothing. You read for momentary excitement, and win nothing of permanent use. You cannot weigh a book. You cannot even talk about a book, further than to say, that you like it or dislike it. The philosophy or the lesson of a novel or a poem is never grasped by you; and every book you read is to you just what Mother Goose's Melodies are to the child, and no more.

You must also perceive a difference between yourself, and those who love society for society's sake. There are many women who love society because of the mental stimulus it brings them—because, in the presence of intelligent and sprightly men and women, they feel themselves brightened and strengthened, and because they find in such society the most grateful opportunity to act upon others. They are talking people who think before talking, and who think while they talk. I have noticed that while you are exceedingly fond of society, you always shun these people. You can talk nonsense, after a fashion, but your special delight is in hearing other people talk nonsense; and the man or the woman in society who says the drollest things, and "runs on" in the wildest way, and does the most to amuse you and to relieve you from the necessity of either thinking or talking, is the one who monopolizes your attention. If you have any special horror, it attaches to being cornered with a sensible man or woman, and being expected to talk sense with them. You see, therefore, that you do not go into society with anything in your hand to pay for that what you receive, except your agreeable person, your willing ears, and your ready and complimentary laugh. These make you popular enough; but are you not just a little ashamed to think that your love of society would be destroyed if you could find in society none but those who have brains and a disposition to use them in sensible talk? Are you not ashamed that all social circles are stupid to you in the degree that they are brilliant to the wise and the intellectual and the ready-witted? Are you not ashamed that the clever buffoon of a company interests you most, and helps you most to what you call "a good time."

You must also perceive that you are very different from those women to whom home is the sweetest spot on the earth. I know many women who have become so much enamored of home that they will never leave it willingly. They never go into society without a sense of sacrifice. They cling to home as if they had grown to it—as if every tendril of their heart-life had wound itself around its pleasant things, and could only be dislocated by violence. This love of home and this self-confinement to its walls and its duties may become, and often does become, an intensely morbid passion of the soul—just as much to be deprecated as an unhealthy love of change—but you cannot but feel that a supreme love of home and devotion to its duties are very lovely, and that the best women you know entertain this love and this devotion far beyond yourself. Your home is not your refuge, so much as the home of your neighbor is. When you wish to be happy—when you feel the need of some soothing and comforting influence—you do not draw the curtains of your home about you, and draw the loved ones of home closer to your heart, but you rush to the house of a neighbor that you may forget your troubles in the diversions of lively society. Your life is not at home. Home is mainly your boarding place; and if there were no such thing as "visiting" to be done, you would feel life to be shorn of most of its attraction. In short, you are never so much at home as you are when you are not at home. You are affected by a chronic mental uneasiness which prevents you from remaining long in any place—especially in any place to which a duty holds you.

I have thus endeavored to reveal you to yourself, by calling your attention to the contrast which you—consciously I must believe—present to four different classes of women worthy to be respected and loved, namely: to those who, by definite purpose, have devoted themselves to a life of active duty at home and in society; to those whose satisfactions are found in culture and its opportunities; to those who love society for the mental stimulus and strength it imparts, and to those who are supremely in love with home and its quiet enjoyments. To one of these four classes, or to sundry or all of them combined, you must know that the best women of this world belong; and I believe that you have sense enough to understand, and sensibility enough to feel that you are not of this number. You are a frivolous woman, constantly on the look-out for new sources of pleasure, and with no definite purpose except to get along as easily as possible with such duties as circumstances have forced upon you, and to have just as many "good times" as circumstances will permit you to have.

Will you permit me now to say, in all frankness, that I believe you to be made for something better than this? You have qualities of body and mind and heart out of which a noble woman may be made—qualities which I cannot help admiring any more than I can help loving the light. Your nature is open and frank, and you will admit at once everything I have said concerning yourself. You possess a pleasant temper and a pure flow of animal spirits, and an affectionate nature, and a general desire that others may have just as good a time as you have. But you get no mental growth, you accomplish no worthy purpose, you are not the steadily radiant centre of a worthy home life. You are not doing a true woman's work in the world, for husband, children and friends, or gaining a true woman's wealth of character and culture. You are, as I have told you before, a child, with children on your lap and at your knee—children who do not very profoundly respect you—children whose acute perceptions have already learned your weakness—children who already treat you like a child. Are you never to be a woman? You ought not only to love home, but you ought to be the abiding corner-stone of home. Your husband's house is not home without your presence and your presidency. That restless mind of yours should have steady work and healthy food. It should have a business—work that will engage its powers in the accomplishment of a worthy object—work that will fill your time and make these "visits" of yours, and these "good times" of yours, the healthy diversions and not the absorbing pursuits of your life. There is a world of life and power in you. It only needs to be held and trained and put to noble, womanly service. I hope you are not so badly dissipated that your will has lost the decision necessary to execute the wish which I am certain now springs in your heart.

If you should undertake reform let me warn you against a mistake that you will be quite likely to make. There are not a few women in the world, considered very useful and pious persons, who are useful and pious in the same way that you are useless and dissipated. They are just as fond of change and excitement as you are, and, being of a religious turn of mind, they seek religious excitements, and suppose themselves to be in the path of duty. They attend a prayer meeting, or make visits to the poor, or wait at a hospital, or go to a benevolent sewing-circle, or distribute religious reading, or minister to the sick, or attend a stranger's funeral, for the change and the excitement which they find in these things. They are just as fond of being away from home as you are, and they seek excitement and amusement for the same reason. I do not think that I entertain more respect for them than for you. Perhaps the sort of dissipation which they choose is preferable to yours, but their motives can hardly be called better. Some of these women neglect their home duties very much, and they do it simply because they cannot obtain in them the excitement and amusement which they seek. Many of them are out on what they suppose to be purely religious or benevolent errands, when they ought to be at home with their husbands and children. Becoming like these women, you would only change your style of dissipation, without essentially changing your motive, or working a desirable revolution in your home-life.

No; you must learn the difficult lesson that in routine lives the real charm of life and the essential condition of progress and growth. That which is now irksome to you, must be heartily recognized as essential to your happiness. You must learn to be happy in the performance of a daily round of duty at home, and learn to be dissatisfied unless that daily round of duty shall be performed. You must learn to take most pleasure in those excitements which flow from action, not passion. These excitements of sensibility in which you have your life are legitimately only diversions from routine. Ah! this routine which is so hateful to you! Why—madam—routine is the road to heaven and God. Routine is the pathway of the stars and the seasons, the song of the tides, the burden of all the generations. The clouds sing it to the meadow, the meadow to the brook, the brook to the river, the river to the sea, and the sea to the clouds again, in everlasting circles of beauty and ministry. Routine is the natural path of all true human life. It is in this path that the feet grow strong and steady, and the soul adjusts itself familiarly to its conditions. It is in this path only that genuine peace and contentment are found; and you must, of stern and settled purpose, hold yourself to this path until you feel the upward lift of its spiral round, and know that you are reaching a calmer atmosphere and a more womanly because a diviner life. Never be afraid of routine. It has in it the secret of your reformation and the condition of your success.

If you could but see, as I see, what a grace thoughtfulness would give your character, and could measure, as my imagination measures, the loveliness that would come to you through the chastening of your wayward impulses by work and self-devotion, I am sure you would fall in love with the picture, and make any sacrifice to realize its truthfulness. It pains me to see you so frivolous, so childish, so incapable of work, so impatient of home restraint and routine, so fond of wandering, so devoted to amusement and play; for I know that the time must come when those animal spirits of yours will droop, when the little delights that now entertain you will become insipid, and when you will learn that your life has been wasted, in a childhood that rotted at last without ripening into womanhood.

THE NINETEENTH LETTER.

To Jefferson Davis Jones, Politician.

CONCERNING THE IMMORALITY OF HIS PURSUITS, AND THEIR EFFECT UPON HIMSELF AND HIS COUNTRY.

THE love of that which we call country is among the highest and noblest passions of the soul. The love that kindles into joyful enthusiasm at the sight of the national symbol, that feels, personally, every insult offered to its object, that burns brightest in absence, that is full of chivalry and bravery and self-devotion, that sacrifices itself on battle fields, and counts such sacrifice a joy and a glory, that lives even after country is lost, and passes down through many generations as a precious inheritance—this, if not religion, in one of its forms of manifestation, is certainly its next of kin. Indeed, there is something of every love, and of all love, in patriotism. Country is the patriot's mistress, his father and his mother, his brother and his sister, his home, his teacher, his friend, his treasure—the storehouse into which he garners all his affections—heavenly and human—all his interests, aspirations, hopes; and when necessity demands it, he turns his face and feet from mistress, father, mother, brother, sister, home, friend, and treasure, and gives himself to his country, in obedience to motives that are hardly to be distinguished from the highest religious feelings and convictions which his bosom holds. I think it would be hard to tell where, in the sublimer walks of the soul, patriotism leaves off and religion begins. In many of its humbler manifestations patriotism doubtless halts this side of heaven, but when it becomes sacrificial, its incense curls around the pillars of The Eternal Throne.

It is to Christian patriotism that we are to look for all the motives which have any legitimate place in government, and the management of public affairs, yet it is to patriotism that resort is rarely made. For the selfishness of supremely selfish men has organized other and baser motives, by which all public policy is fashioned. The love of power and the love of office and the love of money have all conspired in the organization of parties, which live upon lies, and which uniformly die, at last, for lack of dupes, or perish of their own corruptions. It is possible, of course, that two equally patriotic men may differ widely in their views of public policy—so widely that their opinions may furnish a legitimate basis for opposite political parties. Theoretically, therefore, political parties have legitimate ground to stand upon, but practically they are a curse to the country. For the love of party has always usurped the place of the love of country. Everything, on every side, is done in the name of patriotism, of course; but patriotism is made subservient to, and is confounded with party interest. Men forget "our country" in their mad devotion to "our side." It has always been so; I fear it will always be so. History makes a uniform record of the fact that however patriotic the birth of a party may be, and however patriotic may be the motives of the people who sustain it, it passes early into the hands of designing men, whose supremely selfish love of power controls its action and directs its issues, solely for personal and party advantage.

Every thorough politician in the world—every man in whom love of party is stronger than love of country—every man in whom the love of power is the predominant motive—is a possible traitor. It matters not what party he may belong to. I make the proposition broad enough to embrace all parties, and believe in it, as I believe in any fundamental truth of the Universe. A politician is a man who looks at all public affairs from a selfish stand-point. He loves power and office, and all that power and office bring of cash and consideration. Public measures are all tried by the standard of party interest. A measure which threatens to take away his power, or to reduce his personal or party influence, is always opposed. A measure which promises to strengthen his power, or that of the party to which he is attached, is always favored. The good of his country is a matter of secondary consideration. His venality and untruthfulness are as calculable, under given circumstances, as if he were Satan himself. I know of no person so reliably unconscientious as the thorough politician, and there is no politician of any stripe that I would trust with the smallest public interest, if I could not see that his selfishness harmonized with the requirements of the service. Therefore I say that every politician is a possible traitor. There is not a man in America who loves his party better than his country, or who permits party motives to control him in the discharge of his duties as a citizen, who would not betray his country at the call of his party.

I introduce my letter to you, Mr. Jefferson Davis Jones, with these statements, that I may the more easily show you to yourself, and justify my opinion of you; for it will be hard for me to convince you and the public of your immorality. The public mind is thoroughly sophisticated on this subject. The public has a suitable horror of gambling with dice and cards, but is quite ready to call those most indecent and immoral games of chance which Wall street plays "operations in stocks." Nay, the public permits these operations to fix the prices of the property it holds in its hands, and, indirectly, of the bread it eats. It is quite as oblivious of the real character of the politicians who lead it by the nose. A clever politician, who manages to keep power in his hands for personal and party ends —who is unscrupulous in the choice of means for securing his purposes—who is not even suspected of a patriotic motive in any act of his life—is regarded with a degree of admiration and esteem. He wins the objects of his desire, and his success crowns his efforts with respectability. Jefferson Davis, himself, finds it for his personal and political interest to plunge the country which has honored him into the most terrible war known in history, and the people are filled with horror at his treachery and his ingratitude. Jefferson Davis Jones, actuated by the same motive, opposes him; and one is just as bad as the other, and owes to circumstances, and not to his principles, the fact that he is not in the other's shoes. If Jefferson Davis Jones, who now prates of liberty and patriotism and sundry party words and phrases, were in the dominions of Jefferson Davis, he would be his most willing instrument, without the slightest change in the ruling motive of his life.

Do you not feel, sir, that this is so? Do you not know that to all intents and purposes you make merchandise of your country? Do you not regard, and have you not for years regarded, politics as a grand, exciting game of mingled chance and skill, at which opposing sets of men play, not that advantage may accrue to their country or its institutions, but that the stakes of power and plunder may be won for selfish use? Of course you know this; but it is not so much a matter of course that you know this view to be immoral, and this treatment of your country sacrilegious. You have been bred to these things among men who were honored and respected. You have learned to gamble for power from men who first used you as their tool. You have learned all the tricks of the political hells. You pull wires, and play puppets, and veil your selfish purposes behind sacred names, and lie to the people whom you make your dupes. Open falsehood, wicked innuendo, cunning evasion, shameless suppression, downright fraud—not one of these instruments do you hesitate to use when occasion demands for securing your personal and party ends. I tell you, sir, that these lies and subterfuges, over which you laugh and jest in private, are outrageous crimes against liberty, against good government, against a patriotic people, against the public morals, against God.

What is this country that you are playing with so

carelessly—whose interests you are making secondary to your own? It is the present home of thirty millions of people—the future home of uncounted hundreds of millions of people, whose destiny is to be shaped and decided in a great degree by the institutions of the country, and the men who make and administer its laws. You cannot tamper with a single human right without awaking the groans of whole generations of men. You cannot cram a lie down the public throat, and manage to incorporate that lie into the public life, without vitiating the issues of that life through all coming time. You and your friends cannot lead the nation into mistakes of theory and practice without leading it into certain and serious disaster. This country, while I write these lines to you, is suffering indescribable evils from the influence of just such men as you. The rebellion which costs us hundreds of thousands of priceless lives, and thousands of millions of treasure, is entirely the work of politicians; and if it should fail to be suppressed, and the national honor should fall short of entire vindication, it will be through the machinations of politicians. The people of this country are patriotic and loyal, and their action will, in the main, be patriotic and loyal, when they are not deceived by you and men like you. We have only politicians to fear. Selfish men have played their games for power over this country too long; and now we have the day of reckoning. Not a man falls in this horrible war who does not owe his death to those scheming politicians, who, in the past, have regarded their country simply as a chess-board on which they could play their game for power.

What is this country that you are playing with so carelessly? I ask again. It is that for which a million men have voluntarily risked all of good that is covered by the name of "life." It is that for which the great and generous have been willing to relinquish home delights, and home pursuits, and fond hopes and expectations, taking upon themselves the burdens of the camp, and yielding themselves to the sad chances of the battle field. It is that for which a nation of Christians has prayed before God with faithful persistence, mentioning its name with tenderest love and reverence, morning and night, among the names they love best. It is the inheritance of our precious children—an inheritance that may be one of honor—that may be one of shame. It is the property of history. Far down the vista of time, I see the man (whom it requires no prophetic eye to see) whose mind will weigh the character of this country, and whose pen will give his judgment record. I see him sitting in the light of a dawning millennium, while the lurid fires that now fill the sky with flame only feebly light the hem of the far horizon. You and I will have been dust five hundred years, when that calm pen shall begin its story—a story which shall determine for all the following generations of men whether you and I had a country or whether we died without one, or whether we were worthy of one,—a story which shall tell whether we wasted our inheritance—whether we bartered it away for party advantage, or saved and sanctified it by our patriotism. This man, so certainly unborn—so certain to live—has this country in his hands to present to the great futurity of the world. He has you and me and all that we hold dear in his hands, and we cannot help ourselves; and this country of ours we hold in trust for him. Shall we betray our trust, and damn ourselves and our country together?

That which gives me most apprehension for the future of my country is the fact that its affairs are in the hands of such as you, and are likely to be. Theoretically, we are a self-governing nation; practically, we are governed by designing politicians. Theoretically, the people select their own candidates for office, and elect them; practically, every candidate for office is selected by the politicians, the candidate himself being of the number, and the people are only used for voting, and for confirming the decrees of their political leaders. For fifty years this country has not been governed in the interests of patriotism, or been governed by the people. For fifty years, patriotism has not ruled in Washington, or in any of the political centres of the nation. Occasionally, a true patriot has been placed in power, but it has always been a matter of accident. Occasionally, a patriot has been "available" for carrying out the purposes of the politicians, in their strife for power. But often imbecility and rascality have been found "available," and politicians have not failed to take advantage of the fact. Selfish party men have ruled the country, and selfish party men are trying to ruin it. It is beyond dispute that the political leaders of the people of this country have uniformly been men without religion, and without even the pretension of religion. When a political man or a candidate for office has been found to be religious, the fact has been advertised as a remarkable one. Look at the great political leaders; then at the lesser ones; then at the whole brood of petty politicians who are their tools and the recipients of their favors. You know that you cannot find, in all the country, a class of men less regardful of Christian obligation, or more thoroughly the devotees of selfish interest.

Yet this is called a Chistian nation! The theories and the institutions of the country are Christian, but the practice and the administration has as little to do with Christianity as possible. Do you and your associates, when laying out and prosecuting a political campaign, ever consult Christianity,—either its dictates or its interests? Are you Christian in your treatment of an opponent? Are you particular to use only Christian means in forwarding the interests of your candidates and your party? Do you push a Christian principle any further than it will pay as a party principle? Do you not uniformly pander to the prejudices of the ignorant, and flatter the vices of the vicious, while, at the same time, you hypocritically pretend to respect the religious convictions of the better elements of society? Do you not mingle with the degraded, and court the smiles of those who live upon social vices, and descend to the meanest tricks to compass your ends? You can have but one answer to these questions. The political machinery of this country—that by which elections are carried, as they always are carried, in the interest of a party—is simply and irredeemably unchristian. It has not in it even the poor quality of decency.

I have talked in a general way to you about these things, because you are only a representative of a class, and because I am more interested in my country than I am in either you or your class; but it is proper that I say something to you about the effect of your political life upon yourself. You have probably seen enough of it to learn that its lack of religious principle is not attributable entirely to the fact that only bad men engage in it. You have learned that many men who have gone into political life good men, have come out of it bad men. You have seen Christian men there who failed to maintain their integrity among the temptations that assailed them. You have seen good men elected to office, by a combination of influences, who, in their selfish desire to retain their places have thrown themselves into the hands of such as you, and have become as mean and unprincipled as any of them. A minister of the gospel, turned politician, will show the degrading power of his new associations quicker than any other man. There has seemed to be an impression in the minds of Christian men that duplicity and trickery are indispensable to a politician, and not only necessary, but justifiable. It has been the practice to recognize other than a Christian rule of action in political affairs, so that, after a Christian man has been in political life sufficiently long, he usually wears out his Christianity. It is impossible for a Christian to go into political life, and stay there as a party man, and join in the operation of party machinery, and retain a conscience void of offense.

How is it with you? I remember the time when you were not only a patriot, but professedly a Christian. I remember when you first held office; and of the Christian patriotism which actuated you in your first party strife I never had a doubt. You worked faithfully and well for what you believed to be the right. The selfish crowd with whom you now associate looked on with approval, because you helped them; but they regarded you as verdant, and knew with measurable certainty that your generous zeal would soon find rest in calculating selfishness. Your term of office expired, and you were in want of office again, and then you found yourself in the hands of those whom you had already learned were unprincipled. They had called on you for money for party purposes—money which you knew would be spent in an unchristian way, and you had given it to them. You became aware that they had placed a market value on your Christian character, and had calculated on the amount that your patriotic unselfishness would add to their capital. You learned then to scheme with them. You grew unscrupulous in the use of means. You learned to regard politics as a game, and you determined to become a player. It took but a short time for you to become an adept, and when you had conquered the political trade thoroughly, you had become a demoralized man. I do not think you a debauchee, or a thief, or a murderer; but you have lost your sincerity, your moral honesty, your Christian purpose, and your patriotism. I can hardly imagine a character more utterly valueless than yours. You have come to measuring everything by a party standard. You look upon every public question, every matter of policy, and every event, as a party man. You belong to that hellish brood of political buzzards who cannot hear of a battle, or scent a rumor of war or of peace even, without calculating first what party advantage can be gained from it.

I suppose that if I were to give utterance to my wishes and my aspirations touching the future of my country, I should be called Utopian. But that which is possible, and that which is desirable on every Christian and patriotic consideration, is not Utopian, and I should be forever ashamed of being scared by the taunt. This country is to be saved to freedom and to happiness and justice, if saved at all, by the Christian patriotism of its people, and by the institution, in the place of party machinery managed by unprincipled men, of some system of popular expression that shall place good men in power, and bad men in prison, where they belong. It is easy for you and your associates to sneer,—easy to say that this is all impracticable, that the people cannot possibly prevent you from pulling the wires, and that, moreover, you will continue to use the people for your own selfish ends, and use them with their consent. I say it is not impracticable, because it is in the line of Christian and patriotic duty, and is not impossible. I say that this change must be made, or we must, as a nation, be forever going through financial revolutions, social convulsions, destructive wars, and all that terrible catalogue of national calamities which attend the management of a nation for selfish ends. The Christian and patriotic men of this nation must rise, under Christian and patriotic leaders, whom they shall choose, and depose the infernal crew with which you hold association, or we must, as a nation, drift along in a state of constant social warfare, to land at last in anarchy. A nation that is governed by its worst men, who have at command its worst elements for that purpose, must go to wreck. Only the nation that governs its worst men, and holds its worst elements in subjection, can live. You must die, therefore, or the nation must die. Which shall it be?

THE TWENTIETH LETTER.

To Dr. Benjamin Rush Jones.

CONCERNING THE POSITION OF HIMSELF AND HIS PROFESSION.

I HAVE abundant reason to hold you in profound and tender respect. Your devotion to me in sickness, your benevolent self-sacrifice among the poor, your sympathy for the young and the weak, your uniform kindness and politeness among all classes of people, and the Christian spirit and the Christian counsel that you have been able to bear into all those scenes of suffering among which your life is mainly passed, have won my reverent affection. I have never heard you utter a coarse word in the presence of a woman, or jest with coarse women upon themes with which your profession makes you unpleasantly familiar. You are a Christian gentleman; and may God bless you for all the comfort and courage which you have borne to a thousand beds of suffering and dying, for all the pleasant words you have spoken to the tender and the young, and for the excellent personal example that, throughout all your life of ministry, has made every act an exhortation to noble endeavor and your presence a constant benediction!

I have noticed, in my intercourse with you, your profound respect for your profession. You have felt that a share of its honor was in your keeping. A light word spoken of it has been felt by you as a personal insult. You have regarded it with more than the love of a lover; you have guarded its honor with more than the sensitiveness and chivalry of a son. You have believed in it, and honestly labored to give to it a high place in public esteem. This enthusiastic love and admiration of your profession, which you have brought down, without abatement, from the days of early study, is accompanied by the most devoted fraternal feeling toward your professional brethren. You guard their honor jealously, and carry more than your share of that *esprit de corps* which holds together the band of physicians of which you are the best member. This love of your profession, and this regard for those who practise it, lead you, on all occasions, to take side against the public in such medical disputes or contests as may arise, and tempt you into positions which compromise your candor and betray your conscience. The only place in which you have shown yourself to the public as a weak man has been in the position of defender of professional incompetency—a position taken simply through an extravagant respect for your profession, and an incorrect view of the duty which you owe to its practitioners. A professional brother, prosecuted for mal-practice, is always sure that you will do what you can to clear him. Any notorious case of incompetent medical or surgical management, which the public gets hold of, and tosses about, to the disgrace of the profession and the physician who is responsible for it, you always take up and treat tenderly. People have learned that you will not patiently hear anything reflecting upon your profession, or those who represent it. This is all true with relation to what is known in the world as "the regular profession." There is a "regular" profession and there is an "irregular" profession. I do not know that your charities ever extended themselves far enough to embrace any member of the medical fraternity who was not strictly "regular." If you have been devotedly friendly to all who have practised in the regular way, you have been uncompromisingly bitter toward all who have practised in an irregular way, with or without regular diplomas. The only bitterness I ever heard from your lips was poured out upon the head of some "quack," or upon quackery generally. I do not think that you ever, for a moment, admitted to yourself that an irregular physician had cured a case of disease, or could possibly prescribe for a case of disease intelligently. You would never admit the most intelligent quack that lives to a professional or social equality with yourself. You have only contempt for the whole brood, and for all who have anything to do with them. You cannot take yourself socially away from many whom you call dupes to quackery, but, in your heart, you partly pity, partly blame, and partly despise them all.

Now, my friend, you are not generally an unreasonable man, and I insist on your taking good-naturedly a few things I have to say to you. I know that you think I have no right to touch upon a subject like this, but, as a representative of the public, I know I have, and I propose to do it. Is the profession of medicine, practised in the most regular way, by the most regular men, so nearly perfect in its operations and results as to deserve the enthusiastic respect which you accord to it? Do you find medicine so uniformly successful and so reliable in your own hands, with the best regularly acquired knowledge to guide you in its exhibition, that you can have any degree of certainty that you are doing the best thing there is to be done? Is the profession of medicine, as it is understood and practised in this country, so rich in knowledge that it can afford to shut out of itself such truth as may flow to it through irregular channels? Is it so successful in the treatment of disease, and so much more successful in the treatment of disease than various forms of irregular practice, that it has a right to condemn without exception or qualification the irregular practitioner, and call him a quack? Sir, the arrogance of the position which medical men assume, in this and other countries, is an insult to the spirit of the age and the intelligence of the people, and has been carried to the extreme of absolute inhumanity. I have known a regular physician approach the victim of an accident, and, when his immediate services were needed, turn away from the wretch without lifting a finger, simply because he saw that he should be obliged to work in company with an irregular physician. I have known an eminent regular physician go a hundred miles to see a patient lying at the gates of death, with a dozen hearts ready to break around her, and turn on his heel without looking upon her face, and leave her to die, not because he did not find a "regular" physician at her bedside, as a regular attendant, but because that regular physician did not happen to belong to a certain medical society!

I repeat that you are not generally unreasonable, and I should like to know what you think of this. I could multiply instances like these that I have given you; and what do they prove? To my mind they prove simply that *esprit de corps* in your profession has degenerated into contemptible clannishness and partisanship. I doubt whether you would decidedly condemn the acts to which I have alluded, and have little question that you would be guilty of similar ones on occasion. You and your professional brethren act as if you believe that you hold the exclusive right to administer medicine and get pay for it, as if you possess exclusively all medical knowledge worth possessing, and as if you mean to maintain your rights against all disputants, by any available means. You are not alone a mutual admiration society; you are a mutual insurance company. You mean to lord it, medically, over the community, and over each other. No man of your profession can step outside of the regular field to experiment and prosecute inquiry without having his heels tripped from under him. Every man must toe the regular crack, or he is at once socially and professionally proscribed. Now I confess that this is spirited and positive treatment, but it strikes me to be out of keeping with the times, and inconsistent with the good of the public. Moreover, what you call quackery and the patronage of quackery, thrives on this treatment. The freely thinking and independent men of your profession leave you, disgusted, and the people rebel.

Why should you and your associates set up for exclusive possessors of medical wisdom? You know very well that all medicine is empiricism, and you know that medicine has made advances only by empiricism.

Your true policy is to take into your hands, and honestly and faithfully try, all those remedies which have received the indorsement of any considerable number of intelligent men. Your duty is to have your eyes constantly open for improvement, and to take it when you can get it. Almost every system of quackery under heaven has been found to have in it some good —some basis of truth—some valuable power or principle, which it has always been the business of the regular profession to seek out and incorporate into their system. No man of sense believes in universal remedies; but because a remedy is not universal it is not, therefore, valueless. Cold water cannot cure every ill that flesh is heir to, but the fact that it can cure a great many of them is just as well established as any fact in natural philosophy. You, however, will not use cold water, because cold water is used by quacks, and because cold water is claimed by some quacks to be a universal remedy. Preissnitz was a quack—regarded and treated by the medical profession as a quack—but the world has recognized him as a philosopher and a benefactor, and after the prejudices against him shall have been outlived, that which he has done for medicine will slowly, and under protest, be adopted into regular practice.

You and your professional brethren have a very hearty contempt for homœopathy, but homœopathy is to do you and your friends good, in spite of yourselves. No man of sense believes that allopathy is all wrong and homœopathy all right, but a man must be an idiot to suppose that a system of medicine which has won to itself large numbers of skilful men from the regular profession, and secured the approval, when compared directly with regular practice, of as intelligent people as can be found in this or any other country, has nothing of good in it. For you, without experiment, without observation, without careful study, to call homœopathy a system of unmitigated quackery, and to hold those in contempt who practise and patronize it, is a piece of the most childish arrogance. This is neither the way of true science nor liberal culture. You may be measurably certain that there is something in homœopathy worthy, not only of your examination, but of incorporation into your system of practice. It has already modified your practice while you have been talking and acting against it. You are not exhibiting to-day a third as much medicine as you did before homœopathy made its appearance. It has killed the old system of large dosing, let us hope, forever. This is a fact; and what you call no medicine at all has at least shown itself to be better than too much medicine, even when administered in the regular way. You say that a homœopathic dose cannot affect the human constitution, in any appreciable degree. A million men and women stand ready to-day to swear that, according to their honest belief and best knowledge, they have themselves been sensibly affected by homœopathic doses, and that, on the whole, they prefer homœopathic to allopathic practice in their families, judging from a long series of results.

Now, what are you going to do with facts like these? You cannot dismiss them with a contemptuous paragraph, and a wave of the hand, and maintain your reputation as a candid man. If you are a free man, and not under bondage to the most contemptible old fogyism that the world ever gave birth to, you will act as a free man. You will permit no man to limit your field of experiment and inquiry, and allow no society or clique to prevent you from extending medical science over all the facts of medical science, wherever you may happen to find them. I am the champion of no one of the thousand "pathies" that occupy the field of irregular practice, and I have alluded to two of them only because they are prominent. I address you simply as a catholic searcher after truth; and I declare my belief that the regular profession of medicine has failed to keep pace with other professions—that medical science has lagged behind all the other sciences of equal importance to mankind—simply because it would not accept truth when it has been associated with the error and the pretension that is so apt to accompany the advent of truth in every field. The science of medicine embraces, or should embrace, all the facts of medicine, and when you, or your friends, proudly decline to entertain a fact because it was discovered by an irregular empiric, you are not only false to science, but false to humanity.

You cannot but notice a growing tendency in the public mind to break away from the regular practice, and to embrace some of the numberless forms of irregular practice. You notice this with pain, and so do I, because I know that if the regular profession were to pursue a different policy, the fact would be otherwise. You must notice with peculiar pain that this defection is not confined to the ignorant and the superstitious, and that, more and more, it takes from you the intelligent and the learned. Why will you be so stupid as not to see that this waning of respect for the regular practice is owing to the bigotry and intolerance of the regular practice? You assume too much—more than you can carry. You assume to be the sole possessors of the medical wisdom of the world. Every man who does not practise in your way, though he may have been a graduate of a regular medical college, you assume the privilege of condemning as a quack; and you deny to him not only professional but social position. You place all matters of professional etiquette before the simplest humanities, and intend by your policy to coerce the public into your support. The rules of your associations are intended to hold their members to the regular field, to compel them to fight all irregular practitioners out of the field, and to force the public into the exclusive support of the regular practice. It is a thorough despotism, and intended to be; and is so discordant with the free spirit of the time that the public rebel, and many are driven into extremes of opposition.

Do you ask me if I am a medical "Eclectic?" No; I am nothing of the kind. I am a catholic, with every prejudice, predilection, and sympathy of my mind clinging to the regular practice. I have a contempt which I cannot utter for all these "completed systems" of irregular practice, which are built upon some newly-discovered or newly-developed fact in medicine. I have only contempt for the broad claims of quackery in every field. When a man tells me that the regular practice is murder, and that drugs are never administered in allopathic doses with benefit, I know simply that he is a fool. And when an adherent of the allopathic school tells me that such and such things cannot be, in the range of irregular practice, which I know have been and are, I know he is a fool.

I write in my present strain to you, because I believe that through what is called the regular practice the future substantial advances of medicine are to be made. Medical science can only go about as fast as you permit it to go. You are too well organized, you have too many schools, you have too much power, to permit any outside organization to get the lead, and to become the standard authority of the world. My doctrine is that you should become the solvent of all the systems, and not the uniform and bitter opponent of everything that claims to be a system. You should make your system one with universal science, one with humanity, and not build a wall around it. When a man gets so bigoted that he can say that a thing cannot be true, because it is not according to his system, he has become too narrow for the intelligent practice of any profession.

The church is getting ahead of the medical profession, very decidedly. It is but a few years ago that Christians of different sects had just as little toleration for each other as the different sects of medical men have now. There was one of these sects that was "the regular thing," and those who departed from it were made to suffer socially. It was in this country, in a degree, as it is in England now. There is the established church—the recognized church—and all the Protestants outside of it are independents. These independents are looked down upon socially, and regarded with a contempt quite as profound as that which you feel for "quacks" and their "dupes;" yet it is coming to be understood in England that the substantial Christian progress of the time is being made by the despised independents, and it is felt that by their influence they are working a revolution in the established church which will, at no distant day, give to it a new vitality and a fresh impetus. You may fight this revolution in medicine, but it is coming, and when it shall come, you will find that what you call quackery will fall before it.

You, possibly, suppose that there are no intelligent and scientific men engaged in irregular medical practice. If there are not, it is the fault of your own schools, for they have been educated in them by thousands; and the practical point at which I aim is this: that you and they shall meet as scientific men, and that as scientific men you and they shall reveal the results of experiment and inquiry in your various fields of observation. I would have you win from them what they have learned: I would have them win from you what you have learned. I would have you and them do this in behalf of medical science, and in the interest of humanity. Until you become willing to do this, you must occupy the position of despots and bigots—a position which no profession, with science in one hand and humanity in the other, can afford to occupy. At present, you are creating quackery and stimulating quacks at a rate which no other policy could possibly effect. The means which you and your professional brethren are employing to keep the medical practice of the country in your hands, are certainly working to defeat your object. You must be more catholic and more tolerant, or your profession, and every human being interested in it, must suffer a range of evil consequences which I cannot measure. The position which you assume of holding a monopoly of all the medical wisdom, all the medical science, all the power of intelligent observation of disease, is a standing insult to the age, and is certain to be punished.

I am aware that I am quite likely to be misunderstood and misconstrued by you, my friend, and by those of your professional brethren who may read this letter. You have been so much in the habit of calling all irregular practitioners quacks and charlatans and mountebanks—of looking upon them all as either ignorant or knavish, or both together, that you will be quite apt to charge me with favoring charlatanry and quackery. I ask you to associate with no knave or ignorant pretender. No man can more heartily despise a pretender in medicine than I do, either in or out of the regular profession; and, between you and me, the question is yet to be decided as to which side holds the preponderance of ignorance and pretension. As between licensed and unlicensed ignorance and pretension, I have no choice. I simply ask you to admit the fact that there are just as good, true, scientific, honorable, and able men outside of the regular profession as there are in it; that all improvements in medicine must come through empiricism; that medical science is one in its interests, aims, and ends, and that the people have a right to demand that the profession which has its most precious interests in charge, shall not place before those interests its own partisan purposes and prejudices. I wish to have you see how utterly unworthy of you, personally, is your professional bigotry, and to induce you to do for your profession what you are so ready to do in all the fields of popular reform.

THE TWENTY-FIRST LETTER.

To Diogenes Jones.

CONCERNING HIS DISPOSITION TO AVOID SOCIETY.

I SOMETIMES think that I am the only person who understands and appreciates you, and the fact I take to be flattering to my discrimination, for all the fools believe you to be a fool. There are comparatively few who know that behind your impassive spectacles there are eyes full of kindliness and intelligence, and that your shy manner and reticent mood cover a heart that longs for love and a wealth of conscious intellectual power that would rejoice in recognition. Few care to study you, but everybody wonders why you shun society. Few go toward you, because you go toward nobody. I never should have known you if I had not, by pure force of will, penetrated the armor of cool indifference in which you have encased yourself. I was determined to find you, and I found you. I was not surprised to discover in you the average amount of humanity, in its common powers and properties, and more than the average amount of sensitiveness and gentleness. So soon as you saw that I understood you, you surrendered yourself to me gladly, and we held communion with one another, heart to heart.

The first cause that operated to make you a solitary man was a sense of your incongruity with the elements of society, or with the elements of such society as was around you. You looked upon the young, and saw them absorbed by frivolities that had no charm for you—engaged in pursuits which did not interest you. There was but little animal life in you, and no overflow of animal spirits; so you had none of the spirit of play; and you could take no pleasure in the insignificant things with which the spirit of play interested itself. Whenever you were thrown among those of your own years, you entered scenes that had no meaning to you, so that you were always oppressed with the feeling that you were out of place. You knew that your companions interfered with your pleasure, and naturally thought that you interfered with theirs, forgetting that they were thoughtless while you were thoughtful.

This consciousness of incongruity could not long be entertained in your sensitive nature without very serious self questionings. You began to ask yourself why it was that you were an exception to the rule that prevailed around you; and the more you questioned yourself, the more sensitive you became, until there was not a feature of your face, or a part of your frame, or a peculiarity of your speech and personal bearing, that was not inquired of concerning the matter. The result was an impulse to hide yourself from observation, and great reluctance to enter the society to which your life naturally introduced you. Your consciousness that there was something peculiar in your temperament was a hinderance to you—it made you awkward and stiff. While you felt yourself to be the possessor of more brains and more knowledge than most of the young men around you, you despaired of appearing to know anything. You had not the secret of self-possession and confident bearing. Many were your struggles with yourself at first, but at length you became habitually a solitary man. You lost the small measure of confidence which nature originally gave you, lost your familiarity with the forms of social intercourse, almost lost your self-respect. You could not bear to be looked at, or spoken to. You retired into yourself, and sought in self-communion or in studious pursuits for the satisfaction which your nature craved.

I have already suggested the character of that poverty of constitution which has made you what you are. You are not a thoroughly healthy man. Either you are very weak naturally, with no overflow of animal life, or, by heavy drafts upon your nervous system, you have expended that life. Work, or study, or both together, have exhausted your stock of vitality, so that you have only just enough for the necessary uses of life. Until men and women rise to a degree of cultivation which few reach, it is not to be denied that social life is made up of, or is carried on by, the aggregate overflow of the animal life of society. It may be a humiliating consideration, but it is true, that where there is none of the spirit of play there is no social life that is worth the name. Youth is generally social because it is playful; and as youth goes on to middle life and old age, it generally becomes less social because it becomes less playful. Playfulness is the offspring of animal spirits. There are some men and women who bubble throughout their whole lives with this overflow, and are always cheerful and charming companions. There are others who either never have it, or who lose it by expenditure in work or study, and who, as a consequence, become taciturn and unsocial. Lambs in a pasture will run races in delightful groups, and frolic by the hour; but the dams that nurse them and seek all day among the rocks for food manifest no sympathy with them. In the healthy constitution, put to healthy work, there seems to be a stock of animal life and spirits sufficient for the individual, and a superabundant amount which is intended for social purposes. You may look the world over, and you will find that all men and all races of men in whom this overflow of animal life is a characteristic are social, and that all men and races of men not characterized by this overflow are unsocial.

Overflowing animal spirits form the stream on which the social life of the world floats. If other evidence of the fact were needed, than that which lies upon the surface, it might be found in the efforts to produce an artificial overflow at convivial parties. A company of weary men sit down to pass an evening together over a supper. They come together for the simple purpose of enjoying a gay and social time. They know very well that, independent of the contents of certain bottles, they have no power of social enjoyment of the kind they seek. They wish to bring back the hilarity of youth, the carelessness of youth, the overflowing joyousness of youth; but this they cannot do because their animal life is expended. So they get up the best imitation they can of the departed motive power, and a very sorry one it is. When the artificial stimulant has worked its work, the company is social enough, and hilarious enough, after a fashion, but the fashion is a disastrous one. It will answer, however, as a proof of the proposition that in overflowing animal spirits is to be found the medium of social intercourse—the menstruum of all social materials. Even when social life starts from a higher source—from the overflow of intellectual life—it is greatly assisted by animal spirits, and those men and women in whom there is an overflow of both animal and intellectual life are, socially, the most valuable and attractive that the world contains.

You must have noticed, even in your limited observation, how much animal spirits will do in making a man—very inconsequential otherwise—socially valuable. You must remember young men and women with ordinary powers of intellect and not more than ordinary personal attractions, who were deemed the life of every party they entered, simply because they had an overflow of animal spirits. If they were awkward nobody minded it—least of all did they care for it. They brought society a vessel full of life, and society was grateful for it. You took into this same society, perhaps, a mind well stored with learning, and natural gifts superior to any, yet the empty pates amused everybody, and set everybody talking, and furnished the means and medium of social communion, while you sat with your tongue tied, or retired in disgust. Now imagine yourself possessed of the abounding animal life which distinguishes some of your acquaintances, united with the intellectual power and culture which distinguish yourself, and it will be easy to see that nothing could restrain you from society. The overflowing man must play, and he will always seek somebody to play with. If he does not understand the conventionalities of society and the forms and manners of social intercourse, he will good-naturedly blunder over them. He will be social, because he must expend that which is in him in play.

I am aware that your case is not like all those which result in self-exclusion from society, but I believe that no case of such self-exclusion can be found in any man who possesses a healthy overflow of animal spirits. I find that the disposition to shun society exists very widely among students and studious men. I believe it is the truth that most authors and writers avoid society, or feel decidedly disinclined to it. Men who thus confine themselves within doors and exhaust their nervous energy in thought and composition, and with no vigor from the open air, are necessarily without an overflow of animal spirits; and they will find themselves disinclined to society exactly in proportion to their sense of exhaustion. Not unfrequently young women who have been distinguished for their love of society and their adaptedness to it lose both on becoming mothers of families, and never enter society again as active members. So it seems that just as soon as the animal life sinks below a certain level, the disposition to play naturally ceases, and the motive to enter society dies.

And now you ask me for the remedy. You ask me a hard question, and yet I believe that there is an answer to it, though a fresh and overflowing supply of animal life is not to be had for the asking. Undoubtedly something can be done by attending to the conditions of a vigorous animal life. Undoubtedly a life in the open air among men would work a great change in you, but circumstances will not permit this, perhaps, and you seek for the next best course.

I have said that overflowing animal spirits form the stream on which the social life of the world floats. To extend the figure, I may say that on this stream some row while others ride, and the relative proportion of rowers and riders does not vary essentially from that which prevails on more material streams. The rowers are in the minority—the riders are in the majority, and if you cannot row you must be content to ride, for it is essential to your spiritual health that you enjoy the air and sunlight and change which only the passengers upon this stream can win. If you possess no superabundance of animal life, you must be content to breathe the atmosphere furnished by others. You may not be much interested in general society, and society may not be very much interested in you, at first, but I am sure that if you enter it and persistently remain in it, you will not fail to discover points of sympathy between yourself and others from which refreshing and enriching influences will be received by you. Society will take you away from your books and break up your reveries, and that is precisely what is needed. You need to be drawn out from yourself and made to contribute something to the life and wealth of others.

If directly entering general society seem too difficult or too distasteful, there are various indirect methods of entering it which are entirely practicable, and which need not be disagreeable. Enter some field of charitable effort, or public enterprise. Whenever a man undertakes any effort for the good of the public, whether in the broad field of Christian charity or the equally broad field of public improvement, he at once comes into sympathy with a certain number of men and women who give him a cordial welcome. It is only a point of sympathy that is needed to make you feel at home in society. Society may be very attractive to you, though you have but little power to contribute to its life, provided only that you find in it those with whom you have been thrown into sympathy. Think of the effect upon your mind of meeting at the bedside of some sad sufferer, or in some hovel of the poor, a man on the same errand of mercy that took you there. You know that you would feel immediately the formation of a tie of sympathy between yourself and him—would feel that he had reached your heart, that you had found his, and that thenceforward you could meet with mutual esteem. Think of the effect of laboring side by side with men and women in any work of Christian reform, or public education, or literary culture. All work of this character, pursued in the company of others, establishes sympathy between the co-workers, and you have only to engage in it to weave around yourself a net of social attractions that must gradually draw you out from yourself.

You must contrive some scheme for meeting society half-way. You are unlike most men who shun society if you do not feel that it does not quite do its duty to you, in not coming after you. You retire into yourself, you take no pains to show that you possess the slightest social value, you do not even exhibit that interest in humanity generally, or in the community in which you live, that leads you to efforts on their behalf, yet, somehow, you feel that society ought to find you out, and bring you out, and make itself agreeable and valuable to you. You may rest assured that society will never do any such thing. I know that you have no native impulse to social communion—that the spirit of play about which I have talked is gone out of you even if you ever possessed it—but that which most men do by impulse or natural desire, you must do by direct purpose, and as a matter of duty. And you must do this at once. The penalty of failure is the gradual dwarfing of yourself and the sacrifice of all power to influence others. You have a laudable desire to be something and to do something in the world, and know that you have within you the ability necessary to accomplish your purposes, but without social sympathy, you will never know what to do, or how to do for the world, and the world will find it impossible to understand and receive you.

THE TWENTY-SECOND LETTER.

To Saul M. Jones.

CONCERNING HIS HABIT OF LOOKING UPON THE DARK SIDE OF THINGS.

I SUPPOSE you imagine that I am about to endeavor to prove to you that there is no dark side to the things of this life, or none worth your attention. You are mistaken. There is a dark side to every man's life, and to the world's life, which I do not think it either possible or desirable to ignore—a dark side that is legitimately a subject of melancholy contemplation. We live in a world of want and disease, of sin and sorrow, of disaster and death. Our souls, that think and feel, that fear and hope, that despair and aspire, are associated with bodies which are subject to debasing appetites, to derangement, to decay, to a thousand modes of suffering incident to animal being. No mind of ordinary sensibility can look upon, or ought to look upon, the evils which throng the path of humanity without deep sadness. No man of humane instincts can realize, even in an imperfect and faint degree, how the earth seethes with corruption, and moral evil vies with physical disorganization and decay in the work of darkness and destruction, without emotions of mingled sorrow and horror—emotions that cannot be relieved by the encouraging reflection that the future promises an early dissipation of the cloud that overshadows the world.

There are several reasons, however, why neither you nor any person should dwell constantly upon the evil that is in the world. The principal one is that no one can regard it perpetually, with anything like a realizing comprehension of that which he contemplates, without morbid depression or absolute insanity. A man's duty to humanity, no less than his duty to himself, demands that he shall not depress his vital tone and weaken his courage by the contemplation of evils for which he is not responsible, and for the cure or relief of which he needs all the strength he possesses, or will find it possible to win. I suppose the angels of heaven, with their quick sympathies, might make themselves most unhappy over the woes of the world, and fill their holy dwelling-place with lamentations, but I do not believe they do, or that they ought to. The woes of the world are not put upon one man's shoulders, and though we may feel them keenly we have no moral right to permit them to affect us further than to make our hearts tender in sympathy, and our hands active in ministry. If dwelling upon the woes of others had power in it to do them good, there would be excuse for it, but it is the idlest of all painful indulgences. No one is benefited by it, while your own misery, thus awakened, is added to that which awakes it, and the world is only the more miserable for your misery. Thus your dejection is not only harmful to yourself, but useless to the world. It is a gratuitous addition to the aggregate of human woe, and widens the field of misery for other eyes.

But these remarks have comparatively little practical application to yourself, or to others prone like yourself to look upon the dark side of things. The men and women are few who are permanently depressed by the habitual contemplation of woes that do not personally concern themselves. I have heard of persons driven hopelessly insane by a contemplation of the destiny of wicked men, and of others whose horror over human condition has plunged them into Atheism, or some other dark form of unbelief, but these are rare cases. Almost all cases of permanent dejection and of habitual refuge in shadow are the result of personal trials, or of personal peculiarities. Various causes have contributed to make you a dejected man. I think there is a natural lack of hopefulness in your constitution. There are great differences among men in this matter. Some, with naturally hopeful spirits, live through a hard life, and see many bitter days, yet preserve their buoyancy and their hopefulness to the last. Others, with a comparatively easy life and surrounded by pleasant circumstances, will grow sadder and sadder until they sink into the grave. Natural temperament is all-powerful to make some desponding under all circumstances, and others cheerful under any circumstances. Something of your condition is due, I do not doubt, to this native deficiency, though I do not think this deficiency so great as to be the responsible cause of your calamity.

Disease is not unfrequently the cause of much of the permanent dejection that afflicts mankind. Hypochondria is not uncommon, and this is a genuine disease that comes under the cognizance and treatment of the physicians as legitimately as rheumatism, or any other disease. And there may exist a general depression of the vital energies in consequence of age, or the disease of some of the organs concerned in digestion, whose legitimate result is depression of spirits. I cannot tell how much your condition is attributable to causes of this character, but I do not doubt that disease has its place among the causes. Still, neither natural temperament nor disease have worked this work alone. They have done something in furnishing favorable conditions for the operation of other causes, without being very active themselves. I have never been able to find in your lack of hopefulness, or in any disease that has been permanently upon you, the reason for that disposition to look upon the dark side of things which has become the habit of your life. You are probably not aware of this habit. You are probably not aware that you never utter a hearty laugh, that you never confess to a moment of genuine enjoyment, that you are never willing to acknowledge that there is anything encouraging in your life and lot, that you have for years persistently believed your health to be in a failing condition, that you utterly refuse to admit that there is any palliation of your misery in any event that affects you. Your friends are aware that you are in very comfortable circumstances, that not a want is unsupplied, that love surrounds you with its tireless ministries, and that, somehow, life has many charms for you; but you wonder at their perverseness, or attempt in various ways to convince them of their mistake.

I have spoken of your dejection as a habit, and I think it is one, which a sufficient power and effort of will can break up. I do not know, indeed, but you have lost this power of will in a measure, but I cannot think that it is entirely gone. You seem to have plenty of reason and a sufficiency of will with relation to other subjects; and if you could have the disposition to apply both to this, you could break up your unhappy habit, I do not doubt. You have a habit of watchfulness against evil, as if you did not intend that Providence should ever catch you napping. You guard yourself equally against joy, as if afraid of being happier than you have any right to be. For many years, you have kept a look-out for death, determined not to be taken when off guard. This watchfulness against evil and against joy, has been maintained till it has become the habit of your life, and made you a miserable slave.

Far be it from me to deny that you have suffered severely by sickness, by early struggles with poverty, and by the loss of those who were near and dear to you. Indeed, the blows of Providence have been neither few nor lightly inflicted; but they have been blows for which a kind Father has provided abundant balm. No shame has befallen you. No dishonor has come to you. Nothing has happened to you strange to the lot of the hundreds of cheerful men whom you meet. I do not doubt that these blows bent you as grief always bends, but there was no sufficient reason for their breaking you. They were not the expression of infinite displeasure, and were not intended to fill your life with gloom. Nay, you profess to believe that all these precious lost ones of yours are in heaven, and that soon you shall meet them there. I think you are thoroughly honest in this belief, and that even your griefs cannot be held accountable for your habit of looking upon the dark side of things, and your persistent discontent.

I look farther back than grief for the causes of your sadness and deeper than disease. I believe that the real and responsible cause of your dejection is the religious training of your early life, and the ideas which you now entertain of God and of duty. God has never been to you an infinitely affectionate Father, to whom you have been willing to give yourself up in perfect trust. I do not question the honesty of your reverence for Him, or the purity of your worship of Him, but your fear of Him is of such a nature that you seem always afraid that He will play you some trick —that He will call for you before you are ready, or that He only bears a joy to your lips in order, for some disciplinary purpose, to dash it away. You do not, like a child, trust Him—give yourself and all your hopes and all your life up to Him. You have no ease in Him—no peace in Him. You are on the constant watch for yourself, seeking to fathom or foresee His designs concerning yourself, and bearing—with your poor, weak hands—the burden which only He can carry without toil. God the judge—God the ruler—God the providential dispenser—this is your God; but

God the everlasting Father, full of all tender pity and compassion, wooing you to His arms, asking you to repose upon His bosom and give up to Him all your griefs and trust Him for all the future, is a strange God to you. Ah! sir! I am more sorry for you in this great mistake and misfortune than my words can tell.

I think you have always felt that it is wrong to be cheerful. Your religion has been a joyless one. You received in early life, I cannot doubt, the impression that no person, realizing the brevity of life, the tremendous realities of eternity, the consequences of sin and the necessity of constant preparation for death and readiness for every affliction, could possibly be cheerful. Naturally reverent and constitutionally timid, this kind of teaching planted itself so deeply in your spirit that a better doctrine, assisted by your own reason, has never uprooted it. To you, the most joyful peal of bells comes only with suggestions of the grave, and the touch of a baby's hand upon your cheek reminds you only of its frailty and its doom. The earth has been literally a vale of tears to you. As you have seen the young overflowing with life and joy, and dancing along a flowery pathway, you have sighed over them with an ineffable pity. You have never dared to set your affections upon anything, for fear that it would be taken away from you, or that, in some way, it would become a curse to you. You have looked upon life simply as a period of discipline preparatory to a better life, whose joyfulness must necessarily be in the ratio of the joylessness of that which precedes it. Life has appeared to you to be only a preparation for death, and religion has been only something to die by.

Now, my friend, I am very much mistaken if it be not one of the special offices of Christianity to release those who, through fear of death, have all their life been subject to bondage—to make the future so clear and attractive that it shall fill the present with joyful content. I know that we are directed to be ready for death, when it shall come; but how can a man be readier than when engaged actively in pushing on the great work of the world, and enjoying all the satisfaction that must naturally flow from the consciousness of a future forever secure?

If your idea and your policy were to become prevalent in the world, the world would certainly become more thoroughly a vale of tears than it has ever been, —more than you imagine it to be. Such prevalence would be universal paralysis. God is not interested, exclusively, I imagine, with the small concerns of individuals like yourself. He watches the life of nations and the rise and growth of civilizations. One generation lays the corner-stone of the state, and a hundred generations rear the superstructure, and numberless lives are swallowed up in the process. Lives and destinies overlap each other, and one continues what another begins. The thread of silk is not cut off because a single cocoon is exhausted. The single cocoon is not missed, and if it were, there are a hundred to take its place. Men do not live to themselves alone—do not live with reference alone to that which, in the Providence of God, may personally befall them. There is a family, there is a posterity, there is a country, there is a world to live for;—there are great enterprises to be engaged in which consult no period of suspension short of the national death or the final consummation of all things.

What headway do you think would be made in the world's educational and reformatory work by men who, like you, think that there is not much use in undertaking anything because death is so very near? Judge for yourself. Are you an active man in any of the great Christian and humane movements of the time? Do you ever dream of putting your shoulder to the wheel of progress? No, sir. You are the subject of mental and spiritual paralysis; and if the world were made up of such as you, it would come to a dead halt. You have lived in your old house until it is tumbling down about your head, because it has seemed as if anything like a permanent repair of it would tempt Providence to take you away from it altogether.

You could tear the old house down and build a new, but life seems so short and death so near that even the suggestion of such an enterprise has appeared impious. You have thought only of him who proposed to pull down his barns and build greater, and of the end that came before the barns were begun. The new garments which you put on are adopted with the sad reflection that you shall probably never live to wear them out, and every chastened pleasure which you put fearfully to your lips is loaded with the thought that you have possibly tasted it for the last time.

What kind of a Christianity do you think this is to commend to a careless world? There can be no question as to the relative comfort and happiness of the worldling and yourself. The careless worldling, so that he have no vice that burns his conscience, is a happier man than you ; and if he be a man of active, benevolent impulses, he is a more useful member of society. This continual thoughtfulness touching yourself, this constant carefulness of yourself, this perpetual watching of events with relation to their bearing upon yourself, cannot fail to make you selfish,—or, rather, cannot fail to shut out the thought of others and of the great interests of the world at large.

I count that man supremely happy who, prepared in his heart for every emergency, and every event, has given himself in perfect trust to the Great Disposer, and addressed himself with a glad heart to the work and the enjoyment of the present life. Such a man makes no calculation for misfortune and watches not for death, but does that which his hand finds to do, knowing that if he does not enjoy the fruit of his labor, others will, and content to take the ills of life when they come. Such a man sees woe only to do what he can to alleviate it. There is light in his eye, there is life in his step. To me he is the pattern Christian of the world. The bright side of things is with him so bright that its radiance quite overpowers the darkness of the other side. He is cheerful because he is free. Is it too late, my friend, for you to be relieved of this load of fear and carefulness and apprehension ? I think not. I believe that this habit of your life can be broken, and that many happy days can yet be yours—days of calm joy undarkened by a single care or cloud, days of heavenly hope and trust, and days of earnest, far-reaching work.

THE TWENTY-THIRD LETTER.

To John Smith Jones.

CONCERNING HIS NEIGHBORLY DUTIES, AND HIS FAILURE TO PERFORM THEM.

NEXT to being a good husband and father, I consider it every man's duty to be a good neighbor. A good neighbor! My heart brims with gratitude as I write the phrase, for memory, by her magic call, summons to their places along the track of the past a line of ministers whose homely and pleasant faces are as familiar as those of my own family—ministers of good to me in a thousand ways, through neighborly kindness. Among this long line of good neighbors, all of whom I remember with grateful delight, there were some in whom the neighborly instinct was as distinct, and characteristic, and original, as the parental instinct, or the religious sentiment; and I hereby modestly announce myself as the original discoverer of this original neighborly instinct. Neighborly kindness has hitherto been regarded as the offspring of a benevolent disposition, but such a theory degrades it. It is a distinct growth from a separate seed, and often thrives in people who are not remarkable for general benevolence. When unhindered and thrifty, it is, in some natures, the distinguishing characteristic.

Before I come to the treatment of your case, I regard it as a neighborly duty to pay tribute to some of those good neighbors whose deeds are forever embalmed in my heart. To that hearty, loving woman who used to flit backward and forward between her humble house and my childhood's home, lending more than she borrowed, and always returning more, bringing in tid-bits of her cooking to me, always sharing her luxuries with the hand that cared for me, watching with us all in sickness, and always declaring that she had done nothing at all, and was, on the whole, ashamed of the unworthiness and insignificance of her offices, my tearful thanks! Though for many years she has walked in white, upon the heavenly hills, I hope it is not too late to tell her that the man does not forget her pleasant words and kind deeds to the boy, and that the son, though he should live to be old and gray-headed, will always hold in precious remembrance her tender service to his mother. To that old saint whom I used to see stealing across lots to carry food and clothing to needy homes, and entering the back doors of those homes with many apologies for his intrusion, my acknowledgments for his beautiful lesson! To that kind woman who had a large family of boisterous boys, and who not only understood that boys had good appetites, but that they particularly liked to gratify them on the night after the annual Thanksgiving, and found attractions at her house superior to any other in the neighborhood, I assume the privilege of returning the thanks of at least twenty men besides myself. And to him who took a young man's hand in trouble, and giving him his faith and the voice of his encouragement, and sacrificing something and risking much, helped him over the hardest spot of his life into the field of his life's successes, my reverence!

Ah! my good neighbors! I did not dream how numerous you were until I undertook to recall you. Throughout all my life you have formed the circle next to that which sits around my heart. I have exchanged my morning greeting with you, have walked to the house of God with you, have met you at your tables and in my own home, have shared with you the work of neighborly charity; and, ever since I can remember, some of the constant pleasures of my life have come to me from you. In the days of darkness, your gentle rap was at my door, your whispered inquiry was constant, your proffered service was always at hand. And when the little form was carried out to be laid under the flowers, there were fairer flowers upon his bosom, that came from you, than have ever grown above it since. You are my brothers and my sisters, to whom I feel bound by a tie almost as sweet and precious as that which binds me to those who fill my home.

Exactly how this rhapsody will strike you, Mr. John Smith Jones, I cannot tell. I do not think you have looked to see whether you could identify yourself with those of my good neighbors whom I have endeavored to recall. It seems to me that you must be conscious that you are different in most respects from your neighbors. You must be aware that most people are good neighbors among themselves, as most people are affectionate parents. The neighborly instinct is as universal as the parental. Let so much as this, at least, be said for human nature: that without respect to creed or culture, men and women are in the main good neighbors. I have never yet seen the place where the offices of good neighborhood were lacking. There is not only the neighborly instinct engaged in this thing, but there is a universal personal pride that fills out where the instinct fails. It is generally understood and felt that for one neighbor to help another in trouble, and for one neighbor to make the path of another neighbor pleasant, is forever a fit and good thing. This being recognized, it is felt that a gentleman will do that which is fit and good, and that, to fail in neighborly well doing, is to fail to approve one's self a gentleman. I think I know many supremely selfish men who are always spoken of as good neighbors. They have a sense of that which is fit and good. They feel that no person who pretends to be a gentleman will fail to do that which is fit and good with relation to his neighbors. They feel that neighborhood imposes certain duties upon them which they must perform, or lose caste, not only with others, but with themselves. They feel that it is not respectable to be a bad neighbor.

I suppose there may be some neighborhoods in the world that have no bad neighbor in them, but, nearly always, though the many are right, there is one individual in the wrong. Very few are the neighborhoods in which there is not one person who is a bad neighbor. In your neighborhood, Mr. John Smith Jones, you are that neighbor. You are always in a quarrel with somebody about a fence. You are always very much afraid that somebody has encroached upon your line, or is about encroaching upon your line. You keep a miserable dog that worries all the horses that pass your house, and renders it next to impossible for anybody, except a courageous man armed with a cane, to enter your door. You keep hens that enter the gardens of your neighbors, and scratch up seeds, and rip open tomatoes, and wallow in flower beds, and make a nuisance of themselves from May until November, leaving nobody in their vicinity in quiet possession of his premises. You will not take care of your sidewalk in the winter, and I have thought that you take a malicious satisfaction in hearing your neighbors curse you as they hobble over the ice in front of your house. You will join with your neighbors in no effort for beautifying your street. Your consciousness that you deserve ill at the hands of your neighbors leads you to suppose that they are all banded against you, and shutting yourself into your own castle, you look out upon the little world of neighbors around you in defiance, and full of the spirit of mischief. You do not care how much you annoy them. You would feel uncomfortable if you did not annoy them, and though your dog and your hens are a perpetual plague to them, let but a pet rabbit stray into your enclosure, and down comes your musket, and the pet rabbit dies.

How far you are to be blamed for this it is impossible for me to say. I have no doubt that it is a legitimate apology for you to say that nature did not endow you with the neighborly instinct. There is really something lacking in you in this respect, and, so far as this want exists, there is an excuse for you. There is a lack in your nature still further than this. You are not sensitive to feel how everlastingly disgraceful it is to you to be at variance with your neighbors, and to do those things which must necessarily make them dislike you. I suppose that if this letter arrests your attention, you will put in the further plea, or disregarding my apologies for you, put in the exclusive plea that your neighbors are quarrelsome, and interfere with you. Let me say in reply to this that I do not believe the man can be found who is always at variance with his neighbors, who is not himself blamable for it. I know men who are accounted good husbands, good parents, and good men—perhaps religious men—who are notorious as uncomfortable neighbors. I know men of irreproachable morals of whom I never heard a neighbor speak a kind word. In such cases the blame attaches to the unloved person always; and if any man who may read these words, feels that, as a neighbor, he is not loved, let him take home to himself the conviction that he is the sinner, and that when he shall be reformed his neighborhood will be reformed. Quarrelsome neighbors are invariably little-minded persons. A really noble mind never quarrels. A really noble man or woman is never complained of as a bad neighbor.

I think you are a worse neighbor than you were when you were less prosperous. Poverty not unfrequently makes an excellent neighbor and an excellent neighborhood. When men and women are engaged in a struggle for bread, and are obliged to depend upon mutual assistance in sickness and the various emergencies of life, they are very apt to be good neighbors. When you were poor, you were a tolerable neighbor, notwithstanding your want of the neighborly instinct and other noble qualities; but since you became an independent man, all your show of a neighborly disposition has vanished. The sense of independence has isolated you, and given your selfish pride the opportunity to assert and maintain its full sway over your little spirit. Your house is in every sense your castle. It stands as coldly and as lonely in the midst of the neighborhood, and seems as thoroughly barred against neighborly approach, as that of Sir Launfal, that

> "Alone in the landscape lay
> Like an outpost of winter, dull and gray."

Your fences are high; your screens are broad; and behind these you sit, and self-complacently make faces at the world. If you borrow of nobody, nobody borrows of you. Nobody goes near you, and you have abundant time to indulge in the selfish contemplation of your independence.

After all, is not this a small and miserable life that you are living? Does it satisfy you? I am prepared to hear that it does, but it would gratify me much to know that you are not so utterly selfish as to be contented with it. Are there not times when you long for neighborly sympathy—when the face of a loving and kind neighbor, looking in at your door, bent upon some office of good will, or even asking a favor, would seem delightful to you? If such times come, then are you not only saveable but worth saving. Sooner or later the time must come to every man who is worth saving, when he will feel that life has no genuine satisfaction outside of the love and respect of those who are around him. Our only satisfying life is in the hearts of others. You may content yourself with your family, but even for the sake of your family—for the sake of holding the respect of your family—you must sometimes long for the love and respect of your neighbors. No despised and hated man, conscious that he has legitimately earned the dislike in which he is held—can long maintain his self-respect; and when this breaks down, even the worst nature will cry out for help. It must be that there are times when it would be a great relief to you to do a neighbor a favor for the asking.

I do not question the sincerity of your belief that you have very bad neighbors. I do not doubt that you honestly consider them the worst and meanest men that ever constituted a neighborhood. I have no doubt that they have shown their worst and meanest side to you, and that, if the men were to be judged exclusively by the aspect which they have presented to you, their pictures would not be flattering. But you should remember that your position and your words and acts have only been calculated to call forth that which is evil in them. They have shown their worst side to you, because you have shown only your worst side to them. You have provoked their indifference, their insolence, their petty revenges, their spiteful remarks, their cold rebuffs, and all their unneighborly doings. What there is of evil in them, they show to you, because you have been only a bad neighbor to them. Suppose, when you first entered your neighborhood, you had been a generous, kind-hearted, neighborly man, opening your house and heart to those around you, entering their houses, and in every possible way showing good feeling toward them, and doing good through various schemes of improvement; do you think you would have seen anything of this unpleasant side of which you now complain? If you have common sense, you know that all your neighbors would have shown you nothing but good will, and that you would have been loved and honored.

Now this good side of your neighbors, which I see, and you do not, you must find. You can find it, and though, for various reasons, it may seem to you now that not one of them is amiable, you may learn that there is not one of them who is not more worthy to be loved than you are. How is it that they love and respect one another, while none of them respects and loves you? Why is it that you are selected as the object of their united dislike? Sir, you are the meanest man of the neighborhood, and yet you have times of believing yourself abused, and of considering yourself the only decent man among them all. You feel that there is something in you that is loveable, and that that something ought to be loved. That something which your wife has found, which your children have found, which your mother found years ago, should, you feel, secure the love and good will of your neighbors. Are you the only man of all your neighborhood who has loveable qualities that are hidden? All these men whom you have come to regard as bad neighbors are a good deal more loveable than you are, but they show their unlovely side to you, simply because you have shown your unlovely side to them. Show the best part of your nature to them, and you will be astonished to see how quickly they will become lovely to you, through the exhibition of excellencies whose existence has been hitherto hidden from you. You have never shown anything but your hateful side to them, and it is very stupid of you to suppose that they will love that.

I imagine that this kind of talk will do you very little good, but there are two motives which I can present to you that you can measure, and that, I am sure, will commend themselves to your consideration. With all your meanness, you are proud, and you feel that there is something admirable in manliness. Now your position as a neighbor is not a manly one, but it is inexpressibly childish. Are you a man, and do you shut yourself within the lines of your possessions, and quarrel about fences, and lines of boundary, and encroachments? Are you a man, and do you rejoice in making yourself offensive to those around you by petty annoyances? Are you a man, and do you stand ready to pounce upon any unlucky child or pet of your neighbor the moment it enters your enclosure? Do you call such things manly? Are you not ashamed of your childishness? The real man is noble. He will himself suffer inconvenience rather than annoy his neighbor. He will suffer wrong rather than betray a small spirit of revenge. He will not permit himself to be degraded by a quarrel that can be avoided by any generous and self-denying act. By acts of justice and generosity he will compel the respect of his neighbors, and vindicate his claim to manliness. You have moral vision enough left to see all this, and sensibility, I hope, to feel that a mean neighbor is no man, but only a childish imitation of one.

The second motive which I present to you is more selfish, even, than the first, and for that reason you can appreciate it better. A bad neighbor has no influence. No man can move society, in any direction, who has lost his hold upon these who are around him. You have isolated yourself, and you reap the consequences in your loss of influence. You are without power upon the world. With all your fancied independence, and with all the power which money gives you, there is not a man who would permit himself to be moved by you. You must become a good neighbor if you would win power over others for any purpose. As it is, you are counted out of every ring, and have no power to call a ring around yourself.

I wish I could, at least, make you and every other man who reads these words feel that an unpleasant neighbor is a nuisance. There is no good reason why the word "neighborhood" should not be as sweet and suggestive and sacred a word as "family." A neighborhood is a congeries of homes, and the home spirit of love and mutual adaptation and mutual help and harmony should prevail in it. Home life itself is incomplete without good neighborhood life, and every man who poisons the latter is the enemy of every home affected by his act.

THE TWENTY-FOURTH LETTER.

To Goodrich Jones, Jr.

CONCERNING HIS DISPOSITION TO BE CONTENT WITH THE RESPECTABILITY AND WEALTH WHICH HIS FATHER HAS ACQUIRED FOR HIM.

YOUR father, by a life of integrity and close and skilful application to business, has made for himself a good reputation in the world, and become what the world calls rich. He lives in a good house, moves in good society, commands for his family all desirable luxuries of dress and equipage, and holds a position which places him upon an equality with the greatest and best. He began humbly, if I am correctly informed, and has won his eminence by the force of his own life and character. I honor him. I count him worthy of the respect of every man; and I find myself disposed to treat his family with respect on his account —for his sake. This feeling toward his family, which I find springing up spontaneously within myself, seems to be quite universal. The world bows to the family of the venerable Goodrich Jones—bows, not to Mrs. Jones, particularly, as a respectable woman, but to the wife of Goodrich Jones—bows not to his children, as young men and women of intelligence and good morals, but as young people who are to be treated with more than ordinary courtesy because they are the children of the rich and respectable Goodrich Jones.

This feeling of the world toward Mr. Goodrich Jones' family is very natural. It is a tribute of respect to a worthy old gentleman, and, so far as he is concerned, is one of the natural rewards of his life of industry and integrity. I notice, however, that the family of Mr. Jones have come to look upon these tributes of respect to them, on account of Mr. Jones, as quite the proper and regular thing, and to feel that *they* are really worthy of special attention, because Mr. Jones commands it for himself. Instead of feeling a little humiliated by the consciousness that they are treated with special politeness, not because they are particularly brilliant, or rich, or well-bred, but because they are the family of a rich and respectable man, they are inclined to feel proud of it. How they manage to be vain of respectability and wealth won for them by somebody beside themselves, I do not know; but I suppose their case is not singular. Indeed, I know that the world is full of such cases, many of which would be ridiculous were they not pitiful.

The thought that you, Goodrich Jones, Jr., are the son of Goodrich Jones, and that you bear his name, seems to form the basis of your estimate of yourself. I have already given the reason why the world treats you respectfully, but that reason need not necessarily be identical with that which leads you to respect yourself. If, owing to some circumstance or agency beyond your control, you were to be suddenly stripped of all your ready money and other resources, and set down in some distant city among strangers, what would be your first impulse? Would you go to work, and try to make a place for yourself? Would you be willing to pass for just what you are—to be estimated for just what there is in you of the elements of manhood, or would you endeavor to convince everybody that you were the son of a certain very rich and respectable Goodrich Jones, and try to secure consideration for yourself by such representation? I presume you would pursue the same policy among strangers that you pursue among friends. You have never made an effort to be respected for works or personal merits of your own. You push yourself forward everywhere as the son of Goodrich Jones—indeed, as Goodrich Jones, Jr. You have not only been content to live in the shadow of your father's name, but you have been apparently anxious to invite public attention to the fact that you do. You have not only been content to live upon money which your father has made, but you seem delighted to have it understood that you can draw upon him for all you want. You seem to have no ambition to make either reputation or money for yourself. On the contrary, I think you would look upon it as disgraceful for you to engage in business for the purpose of winning wealth by labor.

Now will you permit one who has bowed to you frequently for your father's sake to talk very plainly to you for your own? Let me assure you, in the first place, that all this respect which the world shows to you is unsubstantial and unreliable. The man who treats you with respect because your father is rich would cease to treat you with respect if you were to become poor. The man who bows to you because your father occupies a high social position, would pass you without recognition were your father, for any reason, to lose that position. Let me assure you that the world does not care for you any further than you are the partaker of the money and the respectability which have been achieved by your father. Nay, I will go further, and say that, side by side with the deference which it shows for you on your father's account, it cherishes contempt for one who is willing to receive his position at second hand. You cannot complain of this, for you place your claims for social consideration entirely on your father's position. The negro slave is proud of the superior wealth of his master, and among his fellow slaves, assumes a superior position in consequence of wealth which is not his own. He belongs to a splendid establishment, and, in his own eyes, wins importance from the association. When his master fails, the slave sinks. No, sir, there is nothing reliable in this consideration of the world for you. You are only treated as a representative of the wealth and respectability of another man, and if he were to become displeased with you, and were to disown and disinherit you, you would find yourself without a friend in the world.

In the second place, your position is an unmanly one. None but a mean man can be willing to hold his position at second hand. I count him fortunate who is born to pleasant and good social relations, and all the advantages which they bring him for the development of his personal character; but I count him most unfortunate who, born to such relations, is willing to hold them as a birthright alone. A man who is willing to keep a place in society which his father has given him, through his father's continued influence, is necessarily mean-spirited and contemptible. Every young man of a manly spirit who finds himself in good society, through the influence of others, will prove his right to the place, and hold the place by his own merits. No man of your age can consent to hold his social position solely through the influence of his father without convicting himself either of imbecility or meanness. If you had any genuine self-respect, you would feel that to owe to others what you are capable of winning for yourself, and to be considered only as a portion of a rich and respectable man's belongings, is a disgrace to your manhood.

I suppose the thought has never occurred to you that you owe something to your father for what he has done for you. He gave you position. His name shielded you through all your childhood and youth from many of the dangers and disadvantages which other young men are forced to encounter. He gave you great vantage ground in the work of life, and you owe it to him to improve it. If your name helps you, you ought to do something for your name. If your father honors you, you ought to honor him, and to do as much for his name as he has done for yours. You have no moral right to disgrace one who has done so much for you; for his reputation is partly in your keeping. It would be an everlasting disgrace to him to bring up a boy who relied solely upon his father for respectability. It would be a blot upon his reputation to have a son so mean as to be content with a name and fortune at second hand. I tell you, sir, that you must change your plan and course of life, or people will talk more and more of your unworthiness to stand in your father's shoes, and express their wonder more and more that so sensible and industrious a father could train a son so inefficiently as he has trained you. When this good father of yours shall die, you will be thrown more upon yourself. You will have money, I presume, and you will still sit in the comfortable shadow of your father's name; but the world changes, and strangers will estimate you at your true value, and those who knew your father will only talk of the sad contrast between his character and your own.

I suppose you are not above the desire for the good will of the world. Well, the world is made up of workers. The great masses of men—and your father is among the number—are obliged to depend upon their own labor and their own force and excellence of character for wealth and position. People do not envy him, because he won all that he possesses by his own skill and industry. He is universally admired and esteemed, and you are enjoying some of the fruits of this admiration and esteem in the politeness of the world toward yourself; but this will not always last. You must mingle in the world's work, and cast in your lot with your fellows, contributing your share of labor, and taking what comes of it in pelf and position, or else you will be voted out of the pale of popular sympathy. The world does not love drones, and you must cease to be a drone or it will never love you.

I suppose it is hard for you to realize that you are not the object of envy among men, but I wish you could for once feel the contempt which your parasitic position excites even among men whom you deem beneath your notice. There are many young men who have been compelled to labor all their lives for bread, that would shrink from exchanging places with you as from a loathsome disgrace. They would not take your idle habits, your foppish tastes, your childish spirit, and your reputation, for all your father's money; and these men, strange as it may seem to your mean spirit, are more respected and better loved by the world than yourself. I say that you are not above the desire for the good will of the world; but, if you would get it, you must be a man. You must show that you have a man's spirit, and that you are willing to do a man's work. No idle man ever yet lived upon the wealth won for him by others and at the same time enjoyed the love of the world.

All this you will find out by-and-by without my telling you, but then it may be too late for remedy. You are now young, but, if you live, you will come at length to realize that instead of being envied, you are despised. You will make a sadder discovery, too, than this. You will discover that you have as little basis for self-respect as for popular regard. Years cannot fail to reveal to you some things which youth hides from you. You will find that the world is busy, that you have no one to spend your time with, and that the men who have power and public consideration are men who have something to do besides killing time and spending money. You will find that you are without sympathy and companionship among the best people, and when you ascertain the reason—for it will be so obvious that you will not fail to see it—you will learn that you are not worthy of their sympathy and companionship. In short, you will learn to despise yourself.

I have already spoken to you of the debt which you owe to your father, for what he has done for you. There are some further considerations relating to your family which I wish to offer. A family name and reputation are things of life and growth. The character which your father has made is a product of life, so grand and far-spreading that his family sits beneath, and is sheltered by it. It is the law of all vital products that they shall grow, or hold their ground against encroachment, by what they feed upon. Food must be constant, or death is sure to come, soon or late. The character of your family—its power, position and high relations—is the product of your father's vital force, working in various ways. Not many years hence, that force must stop its work. Your father will die, and unless you take up his work and do it, this family character will pine, and dwindle, and ultimately sink in utter decay.

Look around you and see how some of the rich and influential old families have died out, because there was no man in them to keep them alive. The founder of the family did what he could, raised his family to the highest social position, gave them wealth, bequeathed to them a good name, and died. The sons who followed were not worthy of him. They were not men. They were babies, who were willing to live upon their family name, and who did live upon it until they consumed it. It is sad to see a family name fade out as it often does, through the failure of its men to feed it with the blood of a worthy life; and yours will fade out in a single generation, if you do not immediately prepare yourself to take up your father's work, and carry it on. It is always pleasant and inspiring to see young men who expect to inherit money entering with energy upon the work of life, as if they had their fortunes to make. It proves that they are men, and proves that they are preparing to handle usefully the money that is to come into their hands. It proves that they intend to win respect for themselves, and to lay at least the foundation of their own fortunes. When I see such men, I feel that the name of their families is safe in their keeping, and that, for at least one generation, those families cannot sink. The desire to be somebody beside somebody's son, shows a manly disposition, which the world at once recognizes, and to which it freely opens its heart.

I am aware that a young man in your position has great temptations, and labors under great disadvantages. We are in the habit of regarding a poor young man, who has neither family name nor influence, as laboring under disadvantages, and in some aspects of his case, we regard him rightly. But he has certainly the advantage of the stimulus which obstacles to be overcome afford. The poor man sees that he must make his own fortune, or that his fortune will not be made at all; and the obstacles that lie before him only stimulate him to labor with the greater efficiency. When I see a poor young man bravely accepting his lot, and patiently and heroically applying himself to the work of building a fortune and achieving a position, I am moved to thank God for his poverty, for I know that in that poverty he will ultimately discover the secret of his best successes.

Your disadvantage is that position and wealth have already been won for you. It is not necessary for you to labor to get bread and clothing and a comfortable home. These have already been won for you by other hands. I do not deny that this condition of things is naturally enervating. I confess that it takes much good sense and an unusual degree of manliness to resist the temptations to idleness which it brings; but you must resist them or suffer the saddest consequences. You must labor in a steady, manly way to make your own place in the world, as a fitting preparation for the husbandry and enjoyment of the wealth which will some day be yours. If you have not those considerations in your favor which stimulate the poor man to exertion, then you must adopt those which I have tried to present to you. You must remember that to be content with a position received at second hand, and to live simply to spend the money earned by others, is most unmanly. You must remember that you owe it to your father and to your family name and fame, to keep your family in the position of consideration and influence in which he has placed it, and that it is certain to recede from that position unless you do. You must remember that only by work can you win the good will of the world around you, or win and retain respect for yourself.

If the disadvantages of your position are great, your reward for worthy work is also great. The world always recognizes the strength of the temptations which attach to the position of a rich young man, and awards to him a peculiar honor for that spirit which refuses to be respected for anything but his own manliness. I know of no young men who hold the good will of the public more thoroughly than those who set aside all the temptations to indolence and indulgence which attend wealth, and put themselves heartily to the work of deserving the social position to which they are born, and of earning the bread which a father's wealth has already secured. You have but to will and to work, and this beautiful reward will be yours.

www.ingramcontent.com/pod-product-compliance
Lightning Source LLC
LaVergne TN
LVHW010538100826
845148LV00001B/224
* 9 7 8 1 4 2 5 5 7 5 9 0 8 *